WORKING OUT LOUD

A 12-Week Method to Build
New Connections, a Better Career,
and a More Fulfilling Life

JOHN STEPPER

WORKING OUT LOUD

PAGE TWO BOOKS

Copyright © 2020 by John Stepper

This edition is based, in part, on *Working Out Loud: For a Better Career and Life*, published in 2015, copyright © by John Stepper

All rights reserved. No part of this book may be reproduced, stored in a retrieval system or transmitted, in any form or by any means, without the prior written consent of the publisher or a licence from The Canadian Copyright Licensing Agency (Access Copyright). For a copyright licence, visit www.accesscopyright.ca or call toll free to 1-800-893-5777.

"Luck is not chance" excerpt on page 23 is from THE POEMS OF EMILY DICKINSON, edited by Thomas H. Johnson, Cambridge, Mass.: The Belknap Press of Harvard University Press, Copyright © 1951, 1955 by the President and Fellows of Harvard College. Copyright © renewed 1979, 1983 by the President and Fellows of Harvard College. Copyright © 1914, 1918, 1919, 1924, 1929, 1930, 1932, 1935, 1937, 1942, by Martha Dickinson Bianchi. Copyright © 1952, 1957, 1958, 1963, 1965, by Mary L. Hampson.

Cataloguing in publication information is available from Library and Archives Canada.

ISBN 978-1-989603-05-5 (paperback)
ISBN 978-1-989603-06-2 (ebook)

Page Two
www.pagetwo.com

Edited by Paul Taunton
Copyedited by Melissa Edwards
Proofread by Alison Strobel
Cover design by Peter Cocking
Cover illustration by Michelle Clement
Interior design by Taysia Louie
Printed and bound in Canada by Friesens
Distributed in Canada by Raincoast Books
Distributed in the US and internationally by
Publishers Group West, a division of Ingram

20 21 22 23 24   5 4 3 2 1

workingoutloud.com

*For those who've felt
there could be more to work and life.*

Contents

Preface

AS PART OF an experiment, a researcher puts five monkeys into a large enclosure where, dangling above a ladder, there is a bunch of bananas. The monkeys immediately spot the bananas and one climbs toward them. As he does, the researcher sprays him with a stream of cold water, then sprays each of the other monkeys.

The monkey on the ladder scrambles off. All five sit for a time on the floor, wet, cold, and bewildered. Soon, though, the temptation of the bananas is too great, and another monkey begins to climb the ladder. Again, the ambitious monkey is sprayed with cold water, and so are all the other monkeys. When a third monkey tries to climb the ladder, the other monkeys, wanting to avoid the cold spray, pull him off the ladder and beat him.

Now one monkey is removed, and a new monkey is introduced to the cage. Spotting the bananas, he naively begins to climb the ladder. The other monkeys pull him off and beat him.

Here's where it gets interesting. The researcher removes a second one of the original monkeys from the cage and replaces him with a new monkey. Again, the new monkey begins to climb the ladder and again the other monkeys pull him off and beat him—*including the monkey who had never been sprayed.* By the end of the experiment, none of the original monkeys are left and yet, even though they never experienced the cold, wet spray, they all learned never to try for the bananas.[1]

This story, loosely inspired by research in the 1960s on "cultural acquisition of behaviors," has become one of those business parables that people share like a cautionary folktale. The story spreads because it captures a truth many of us can relate to, a truth I observed time and again in the companies where I worked. Of course, not every workplace is a cage and not every boss is an evil scientist, but enough of us have been sprayed with cold water that we dampen our ambitions and aspirations, and everybody loses.

I wrote *Working Out Loud* because I found a way to stop this negative cycle, a way to take more control of your career and life no matter what environment you're in. Since then, Working Out Loud (or WOL, for short) has developed into a growing movement made up of individuals who want something more than "just a job."

People who love the feeling WOL gives them often want others to experience it too. They volunteer to organize meet-ups and WOL Conferences ("WOLCONs") and to spread WOL inside their companies. They've translated the method into ten languages. As a result of their efforts, the method described in this book has been used by people in over sixty countries.

They come from a wide range of work environments and cultures: employees in large corporations, freelancers, factory workers, nurses, students. What do they all have in common? A woman in Shanghai summed it up: "People are Working Out Loud not just because we're fans of the method, but because we're hungry for a taste of what work could be like."[2]

Work *can* be better. You deserve it and the world needs it. Working Out Loud can help you experience it.

JOHN
January 2020
New York City

Introduction

"JOHN, WE HAVE to make a change."

As soon as I got to his office, I knew something was wrong. My boss had arranged a special one-on-one meeting with me for early Monday morning. The first thing he said when I sat down was that my area was being reorganized. "If you can find a new role in the next sixty days . . ." He didn't need to finish that sentence. I sat there, stunned. I could feel the blood rush to my face. Throughout the rest of the short meeting, all I could think was, *Why? What if I can't find a new role?* and, *What will I tell my wife?* I left his office humiliated, angry, and afraid.

Walking home, I realized how tenuous my position was and how little control I had. I was in my forties and had few meaningful connections that could help me. My confidence was at an all-time low. I knew the job market was terrible, and the prospect of looking for work left me anxious and depressed. Eventually, I wound up finding

1

another assignment elsewhere in my department, one with less responsibility, less status, and less pay.

Up until the meeting with my boss, I had been lucky. Good projects. Powerful sponsors. The right place at the right time. Then my luck ran out. I had been playing career roulette my entire life and didn't even know it. Looking around me, I noticed that almost everyone else was playing career roulette too. Each time you get a new boss or there's a reorganization, it's like a spin of the wheel. The lack of control causes smart, capable people to become scared and defensive, more competitive with colleagues, and less kind.

I figured there must be a better way, and I began searching for it.

A small step

In the beginning, I was just trying to find my own voice, getting in touch with what it was I wanted to contribute and how I might offer it. Looking for a kind of outlet as I was changing roles, I began using a low-tech blogging platform that was available inside the company. I wrote about the work I was doing, what I was learning, and ideas for future projects. One post attracted over a thousand comments. Another resulted in a senior business leader I didn't know reaching out to me to exchange ideas. Over time, more people from other areas in the firm started approaching me for my opinions, sometimes suggesting ways we could work together.

Something clicked. I saw that by making my work visible, I was shaping my reputation and getting access to opportunities I wouldn't have known about otherwise.

A powerful kind of networking

Still conscious of my lack of meaningful connections, I enrolled in a course called the Relationship Masters Academy. The course was taught by Keith Ferrazzi, the author of *Never Eat Alone* and *Who's Got Your Back*. During the course, we formed small peer support groups to practice what we were learning. I was in a group of successful bankers, which intimidated me, and in our first session we were instructed to share something intimate about ourselves. Ferrazzi told us to avoid small talk and instead share something that few people knew and that would expose our vulnerability, something that would humanize us and make people care. One person talked about growing up as a poor immigrant and about his difficult relationship with his father. Another talked about his divorce. Sharing these facts about ourselves changed the intimidating bankers into people I could relate to and care about, and we continued to meet long after the course ended.

This is not normal. At work, most of us feel compelled to hide behind a mask of cool professionalism. I was *trained* to hide behind that mask. As a result, we're reduced to an impersonal sameness, and the chances for human connection are greatly reduced. In Ferrazzi's course, I learned that not only is it okay to be more authentic at work, it also leads to better relationships and greater collaboration.

Purposeful experiments

The combination of my visible work and my growing network made feel like I had more control and motivated me to try new things. I began sharing more of my work publicly, writing in the evenings and on weekends. I applied to speak at conferences as another way to develop my reputation and network. I looked for ways to collaborate with people inside and outside the company.

Because what I was doing was visible, support for it was also visible, and that eventually convinced my management to create a new kind of role for me, one focused on improving how employees communicated and collaborated. Our team introduced a new collaboration platform into the company, and it became one of the biggest internal social networks in financial services.

My mindset shifted. Instead of focusing on making my boss happy and preserving my place in the organization chart, I started to look at work as a kind of laboratory, where I could experiment and learn, where I could improve my skills while doing work that had more impact. For the first time in my life, my job was fulfilling.

A setback and a way forward

Eight years after that meeting with my boss, a different manager told me my job was "restructured," a clinical way to say I was being laid off. The bank where I worked had been struggling on many fronts, and someone decided I was no longer needed. After nineteen years with the company, my grand exit was a few minutes in a conference room with someone from Human Resources. My manager dialed in via speakerphone.

This time, though, my reaction was different, because I had been Working Out Loud.

I had gradually developed relationships with people around the world who knew me and my work and were interested in what I was doing. These relationships gave me a sense of connection and purpose. They also gave me access to knowledge and opportunities. Just a month before I got my severance letter, I had the chance to deliver a TEDx talk about WOL.[1] A few weeks after I packed up my office, I was at Bosch, in Stuttgart, giving a presentation to a global audience—my first bit of revenue as a one-person start-up. Following that were talks at Daimler, Siemens, and BMW. The elements of Working Out Loud, which I'll describe in Part II, led me to more opportunities. I felt, perhaps for the first time, that I wasn't playing career roulette anymore.

Putting the elements into practice

While I was still working in a big company, the elements of WOL had made for a better approach at work, and I wanted to see how I could help others use that approach. I conducted more experiments, made a lot of mistakes, and gradually distilled what I learned into a method that anyone could put into practice: Working Out Loud Circles.

A WOL Circle is a confidential peer support group of four or five people. You meet for an hour a week for twelve weeks, following simple guides to make progress toward individual goals you each choose at the beginning, and to build relationships related to that goal. By the end of the twelve weeks, you have a bigger network, better communications skills, and more confidence. Part III of this book provides stories, examples, and exercises that can help you practice WOL for yourself. If you decide to join a Circle, everything you need is at workingoutloud.com.

You might use your WOL Circle to accomplish something specific, learn about a topic, or explore what could give your work and life greater purpose. You might use it to find a new job or discover ways to make more of the job you already have.

You might also use Circles to change your company's culture. There are now grassroots WOL movements in hundreds of organizations, and some have scaled to thousands of people. For these companies, Working Out Loud complements their HR and culture change programs by tapping into intrinsic motivation for behavior change. For both employees and the company, it's a way to rehumanize what work has become.

When I ask people in a WOL Circle for one word to describe how they feel after the twelve weeks, the most common response is "empowered." Imagine that you felt more empowered, more confident. Imagine you could build meaningful relationships that make you more effective and earn you access to more opportunities. What would you do? Where would you go?

Let's find out.

PART I

For a Better Career and Life

1

Four Stories

Chance favors the connected mind.

STEVEN JOHNSON,
Where Good Ideas Come From

THE FOUR PEOPLE in this first chapter come from different backgrounds and vary in terms of education and social skills. They're at different stages of their lives and careers. Three were in Working Out Loud Circles, and all share an approach to work and life that makes them more effective, earns them access to a wider range of opportunities, and increases their chances of finding meaning and fulfillment in what they do.

Sabine writes her own next chapter

After more than twenty years of working in Human Resources for Siemens, Sabine was ready for a change.

For the most part, she liked the work there: the people, the projects. She just felt there was more she could offer. While she worked in Learning & Development on creative ways to train people, she also had ideas about leadership, corporate culture, and the influence of digitalization. Unfortunately, those ideas didn't fit neatly into her role in the hierarchy. She had a clear sense that if she strayed too far outside the lines she would get into trouble of some kind.

It was time for something different, but what? Sabine was in her late forties, and if she looked for a job somewhere else, given her age and experience, she would almost certainly be pigeonholed into a similar role. She had other interests she might pursue, but none felt like next steps in her career.

So Sabine decided to stay where she was, and started doing small experiments instead. She began reaching out to start-ups in a Siemens accelerator program in Berlin to learn more about what they do and how they do it. That inspired her to try her own small start-up on the side, restoring Scandinavian furniture, just to see if she could make a living without the safe job she had. (She couldn't.) She searched for tools and trends in Human Resources, one of which was a new personal development method. She tried it, liked it, and started to spread it amongst her colleagues. These experiments helped her develop new skills and attitudes, and boosted her confidence. She became known as a kind of "HR Scout," the person who would explore new areas and share what she learned with her colleagues, all without asking for permission or budget.

And she started to write. At first it was on the company's social intranet, where anyone could post an article or comment. Later, it was on LinkedIn. Over time, Sabine began writing on the full range of topics about which she cared and had insights, and those posts helped her establish connections inside and outside the company. Making her work visible gave her access to more ideas and learning, while also emboldening her. Where she used to only attend conferences, now she began to deliver presentations at some of them. "I realized that I have something to give that wasn't being used by my employer but is valuable for others," she said. "It's a great experience, one you would not expect to have when you're in your forties or fifties."

Sabine developed personal relationships with people at companies across Germany, who came to know and like her for what she thought and did, not for where she worked. As her network expanded, so did her range of options. For example, she wound up collaborating with seven companies on a project related to the personal development program she introduced at Siemens. The way they worked together was so extraordinary that they won an HR Excellence Award for Employee Engagement and Collaboration, the first time it was ever awarded to a group of companies.

The learning from her experiments and relationships helped Sabine identify her next step, and she joined her husband in his independent consulting company. Now she delivers keynote presentations and workshops to companies and conferences across Europe on employee development and leadership practices, the new role of HR, and the future of work. She and former colleagues were recognized with a XING New Work Award. She has been honored as a Top Voice on LinkedIn, listed as one of the top 25 HR influencers in Germany's premier Human Resources magazine, and named one of the "40 Top HR Minds" alongside the CHRO of Siemens, her former boss's boss's boss's boss's boss.[1]

Sabine is no longer defined or limited by the box she was in—"Sabine from Siemens HR"—or the track she had been on for so long. Instead, she found her voice, discovered her own path, and shaped her future, enabling her to access possibilities she couldn't have imagined even a few years earlier. "Step by step," she told me, "you take back control of your own life."

Anja earns access to more possibilities

Anja grew up in a picturesque small town of fewer than fifteen thousand people. Upon graduation from the local high school, she applied for an internship at a savings bank about fifteen minutes away. She got the job.

After four years, Anja knew she wanted more from work but didn't think she could get very far without a university degree. So she enrolled in a college with an evening program, and for several years she juggled working during the day with going to classes and studying at night. Meanwhile, as it became clear that a career in a local bank wasn't going to be enough for her, she moved to a large company in a nearby city and got an entry-level job as a clerk in the Purchasing Department.

When she finally graduated, though, after all those nights and weekends of extra work, she was offered a role as a secretary. It was disappointing. She said, "All that effort to get a degree just to sit there in the end and stick receipts on my boss's expense report made me more and more frustrated every single day." Then she paused and slowly repeated that last phrase, as if reliving it: "Every. Single. Day."

It wasn't that she thought being a secretary was beneath her or was necessarily a bad job. She just felt she could contribute more. "I wanted a job where I could bring in my passion, where my talents could be seen, and where they would be useful for the company at the same time." Although her new company had many, many jobs that might be more meaningful or fulfilling, she had no idea how to show she was qualified for them, or to get any extra experience she might need. Although Anja was only in her early twenties, she began to feel stuck.

Being a secretary is usually a behind-the-scenes kind of job, where few people other than your manager know what you do, how well you do it, and what else you're capable of. But Anja figured out a way to make herself and her work visible. She had seen that the company was promoting their internal collaboration tools and that a "digital transformation" was part of the corporate strategy. So, she started a blog and called it "How to work digitally as a secretary."

She began by writing about the tools and techniques she used to be more efficient and effective. The point wasn't to show off, but to be genuinely helpful. A few people read her first posts, then a few more. She started to get comments thanking her for the tips she was sharing, and wanting to know more about her approach and how she handled her work. Gradually, her writing began to attract thousands of views, and was shared by colleagues she didn't know. Her network started to grow. "People started to consider me an expert," she said. One of the people who took notice of what Anja had to offer was her boss, who offered her a different role.

Anja moved from being an assistant in the Purchasing Department to being a community manager for two online groups in the division. From there she took on the title of "agile coach," conducting training, coaching individuals, and facilitating workshops. Now she regularly acts as a mentor for teams, departments, and leaders, and she actively promotes digital collaboration and networking throughout the division. Recently, she organized a huge cross-company conference, and shared the stage with two board members.

"It wasn't easy," she said. "But it was worth it. I can now show my talents, and live my passion, in my new job." Anja no longer feels stuck or invisible. Instead, she has found a way to realize more of her potential, and it feels like a new beginning.

Mara creates a new kind of job

Despite having a wide range of skills, speaking multiple languages, and spending years living in places from Croatia to New Zealand, Mara found herself in what she described as "the worst job possible"—configuring Lotus Notes databases in a big corporation. The work was both tedious and isolating, and few people seemed to know or care about what she did. Nevertheless, she didn't want to change companies again. She just wanted a better role.

Her first step toward a different approach was when she started using the collaboration tools at her firm. She liked the interaction online and the ability to discover people across the company who shared her interests. When she used the tools to participate in an online community, like Sabine and Anja did, she became interested in how to make the community better and began doing research and talking with experts. As she learned more about how to organize successful online communities, Mara shared her work so others could create their own groups. Over time, that helped her develop a reputation as an expert in communities and collaboration, which led to a full-time role as the head of a collaboration team. Though still at the same company, she went from the worst job possible to a job she genuinely loved. She noted that the process of finding the new role was unlike anything she had yet experienced: "Usually you go through the available jobs and try to get picked for one. But I created the job. And it evolved as I learned more about what it could be. It's the complete opposite of what you normally do. It's like being able to write your own job description. You become the job. I didn't know that was possible before."

As Mara built communities at work, learning by doing, she found she had more to say. She started to speak in public, though it took a while to overcome her reservations. "I didn't feel like an expert. Who am I to speak to these people? But when I talked to more people, I realized I knew more than I gave myself credit for." She went on to speak at major conferences in Paris, Sydney, and Berlin. She lectured at Imperial College London and spoke at countless events at her company. People at all levels recognized her as an expert. Later in this book, you'll learn how she connected with CEOs and a former prime minister as she continued to work in an open, generous, connected way. Because of her learning, her contributions, and her purposeful networking, Mara now has more possibilities than ever. She could stay at her company, broadening her expertise by working with different businesses, or she could leverage her network to access different roles in different organizations in different industries.

Jordi Muñoz becomes a CEO

I came across the remarkable story of Jordi Muñoz during my research. He was born in the coastal city of Ensenada, Mexico, about seventy-five miles south of San Diego. His English was limited, and he didn't go to college. In his late teens, still waiting for his green card after moving to the United States, he found out he was going to become a father.

What do you think of his chances for finding fulfilling work?

Like most of us, Jordi started out with dreams of what he wanted to be when he grew up, and he tried to map those dreams to jobs he knew about. "I was very obsessed with airplanes since I was four years old. So I was always dreaming to be a pilot or probably an airplane mechanic," he told ABC News.[2] As he got older, he began playing with computers and remote-controlled airplanes as a hobby. At nineteen, he joined an online community where hobbyists could share information and learn from each other. There, Jordi made his work visible by contributing designs he came up with. "I made an autopilot for my RC [remote-controlled] helicopter with accelerometers extracted from the nunchuck of a Nintendo Wii," he says in Chris Anderson's *Makers*.[3] He apologized in his online postings for his poor English, but other hobbyists cared more about his designs.

Chris, a best-selling author, speaker, and former editor of *Wired* magazine, had started that online community. He had become interested in drones as a hobby, and then decided to start DIYdrones.com so he and other hobbyists could share what they were working on and learning. In *Makers*, Chris describes how he first noticed Jordi in that community based on the designs he was contributing. Over time, Chris corresponded with him, and eventually they collaborated on several projects. When Chris later decided to start a robotics company, he asked Jordi to co-found it, and it was only then that Chris learned about Jordi's background.

Normally it would have been ludicrous for Jordi Muñoz to apply for a job as CEO of a robotics company. He didn't have a university degree to certify what he knew, and his resume wouldn't have attracted any attention from a recruiter or on LinkedIn. There would simply be no way for his application to reach someone like Chris Anderson or to stand out if it did. But Jordi was able to shape his reputation based on his work, his passion for it, and the value other people saw in it. Jordi's contributions to the online community helped make him and his work visible, enabling him to gradually develop a set of relationships that unlocked opportunities.

Four different people. One approach.

These four people, along with dozens of others you'll meet throughout the book, all developed an approach that gave them more control, as well as more options.

Sabine, Anja, and Mara all used a Working Out Loud Circle to learn new skills, build their network, and earn access to new opportunities, while Jordi took charge of his career without taking part in a Circle or even knowing the phrase "Working Out Loud." The aim of the rest of the book is to enable you to develop this kind of approach yourself, using a Circle or not, so that you can have the power and ability to improve your career and life in ways that matter to you.

2

Improving Your Odds

Luck is not chance—
It's Toil—
Fortune's expensive smile
Is earned

EMILY DICKINSON

MUCH TO MY embarrassment as a child, my mother would try to guess a person's zodiac sign when she first met them—"You're a Gemini, aren't you?" She was a big believer in Fate. Some people, she figured, were born under a lucky star, and some weren't.

I always saw this as grossly unfair. For sure, some of us come into the world with more advantages than others, but as a kid growing up in a poor family in the Bronx, I desperately wanted to believe that I had at least some control over my path through life. I wanted to believe I could earn "Fortune's smile."

But what, exactly, did I need to do?

How we feel about work

In the early 1970s, Studs Terkel sought to understand our relationship with work. He traveled across the United States, interviewing over a hundred people in a wide range of jobs, from gravedigger to TV executive, and published the results as *Working: People Talk About What They Do All Day and How They Feel About What They Do*.[1] The book consists almost entirely of the words of the people he interviewed, and what they have to say is incredibly poignant.

I think most of us are looking for a calling, not a job. Most of us . . . have jobs that are too small for our spirit. Jobs are not big enough for people.

That's the thing you get in any business. They never talk about personal feelings. They let you know that people are of no consequence.

It was almost like a production line. We adjusted to the machine. The last three or four years were horrible. The computer had arrived . . . I had no free will. I was just part of the stupid computer.

Many people felt stuck, like they had few options and didn't know what to do about it.

I don't know what I'd like to do. That's what hurts the most. That's why I can't quit the job. I really don't know what talents I may have. And I don't know where to go to find out.

A lot has changed since then, of course. The population of the world has almost doubled. We have the internet, and an array of technologies that seemed like science fiction when I was a kid. Yet, at work, it feels as though we're still looking for the same things.

More than forty years after Studs Terkel's interviews, Bob Chapman talked to a new generation of workers. Chapman is the CEO of Barry-Wehmiller, a 130-year-old manufacturer of machines that do things most of us never think about, such as injecting shampoo into bottles or making toothpaste boxes. (It may not sound exotic, but Barry-Wehmiller's financial performance is on par with Warren Buffett's.) In *Everybody Matters*,[2] Chapman writes that he is "completely obsessed with creating a culture in which all team members can realize their gifts, share those gifts, and go home each day fulfilled." Yet it was obvious to him that most of his eleven thousand employees had a very different experience each day. To learn what needed to change, he would ask employees how they felt about their work, and he included what they told him in his book:

Do you know what it's like to work in a place where you show up every morning, you punch a card, you go to your station, you're told what to do, you're not given the tools you need to do what you need to do, you get ten things right and nobody says a word, and you get one thing wrong and you get chewed out? You feel empty. That was basically every day.

We had four supervisors who circled throughout the work areas all day, making sure everyone was working. There was very little information sharing because they didn't feel we needed to know much . . . we blamed each other for the problems we had. It was old-school manufacturing: You came to work every day, didn't ask any questions or make any waves, and made sure that you got your work done.

Do you know what it's like to feel like you have to put a mask on at work?

Despite all of the advances since Studs Terkel wrote *Working*, many of the themes remain the same: we want to be seen and respected, to contribute and learn, to see some kind of meaning in what we do. Even if we say, "It's just a job," we want more. Terkel summarizes it this way:[3]

Work is about a search, for daily meaning as well as daily bread, for recognition as well as cash, for astonishment rather than torpor . . . for a sort of life rather than a Monday through Friday sort of dying.

Why isn't it getting better?

The employee engagement reports from Gallup are oft-cited evidence that most of us experience "a Monday through Friday sort of dying." Gallup has surveyed more than twenty-five million US workers in different kinds of jobs since the 1990s. Their "State of the American Workplace" asserts that "70 percent of the workforce is checked out." Even worse, people are "acting out their unhappiness and undermining others."

In a *New York Times* article, Tony Schwartz and Christine Porath describe a similar study with similar results.[4] In partnership with the *Harvard Business Review*, they surveyed twelve thousand mostly white-collar workers and found the majority didn't have a sense of meaning and significance, opportunities for learning and growth, opportunities to do what they do best, or a connection to the company's mission. The researchers labeled the modern workplace a "white-collar salt mine." One dispirited commenter said, "I feel worse after reading these comments, because it seems to be the same everywhere."

Why isn't it getting better? Part of the reason is that the way we work hasn't changed much in the past hundred years. In *Brave New Work*, Aaron Dignan describes it this way:[5]

If I showed you a house, a car, a dress, or a phone from 1910 and asked you whether it was modern or antique, you'd have a pretty good idea. Because almost everything has changed. But not management. Somehow, amid a period of relentless innovation...the way we come together as human beings to solve problems and invent our future has stayed remarkably constant.

At large companies in particular, work has become increasingly dehumanized, more about processes and systems than about people. As Maddie Grant and Jamie Notter say in *Humanize,* "we run our organizations like machines,"[6] and we've been stuck with a mechanical model of corporations for over a century. While Scientific Management and its focus on automation and optimization has yielded tremendous progress in many respects, it has created work environments that human beings increasingly dislike.

Think of your last performance review, or when a manager, system, or process prevented you from doing what you thought was best, or forced you to do something you thought was pointless. Think of the acronyms and numbers your company uses to define each person's position and level in the organization. How do these things make you *feel*?

It's not news to management teams that many employees don't love what they do, and most leaders want to do something about it. There's plenty of evidence that how individuals feel about work correlates with the overall business performance of the company. The Gallup researchers, for example, found that engagement at work correlated with improved performance in *nine different work categories,*[7] from profitability and productivity to customer satisfaction and safety. When compared to actively disengaged employees (20 percent of the workforce), engaged staff have fewer accidents, fewer defects in their work, and even lower health-care costs. Gallup estimated the cost of actively disengaged employees at around half a trillion dollars annually. When you feel better about work, it helps both you and your company.

We know we need to change how we work, but most of us don't know how.

Your job might not be the problem

One of the curious things about what Studs Terkel uncovered in his interviews was that people found satisfaction (and dissatisfaction) in all sorts of jobs. Happiness at work seemed to be determined more by the environment—the people, physical environment, systems, and processes—than by the specific role.

In the late 1990s, a team of researchers led by Amy Wrzesniewski (rez-NEFF-skee) sought to test this idea, asking people in clerical and professional jobs how they viewed their work.[8] The researchers asked:

- Is your work just about money?

- Is it about a deeper personal involvement where you mark achievement through advancement?

- Do you take pleasure in the work itself and the fulfillment that comes from doing it?

In short, do you view your work as a job, a career, or a calling? Surprisingly, the answers were evenly distributed for people doing the same kind of role. How you view your work "could not be reduced to demographic or occupational differences," said the study. So the researchers concluded it must be something else that makes us view similar roles so differently.

What is this "something else"? It's our intrinsic motivation. In the last few decades, behavioral research has given us greater insight into what motivates human beings as a species. It has led to what professors Edward Deci and Richard Ryan call "Self-Determination Theory," which was popularized in *Drive: The Surprising Truth About What Motivates Us* by Daniel H. Pink. He sums it up in a few sentences:[9]

We have three innate psychological needs—competence, autonomy, and relatedness. When those needs are satisfied, we're motivated, productive, and happy. When they're thwarted, our motivation, productivity, and happiness plummet.

We are wired to want a sense of control, a sense of competence or progress, and a sense of connection to people as well as to a purpose. Your drive—your motivation to do something and how you feel about doing it—is based on whether or not you're meeting these psychological needs. It's important to note that this is highly subjective and personal. Do you feel like you're in control of what you do each day, or how you do it? Do you feel you're learning and getting better at what you do? Can you relate to your company's purpose, or to the people who work there? If a factory worker taps into their drive while a surgeon doesn't, the factory worker will likely feel better about work than the surgeon does.

The findings of Wrzesniewski and Terkel are good news because they show that, almost no matter what job you have, you don't have to feel stuck. You have more control than you might think. The rest of this book is about how to improve your odds of tapping into your drive at work. One way is to change your approach to your current job, increasing your sense of control, learning, and feeling of relatedness. Another way is to build a network of relationships that gives you access to other environments—a different role, boss, company, or kind of work—where it might be easier for you to tap into your drive. Working Out Loud helps you implement both strategies.

Strategy #1: Start where you are by crafting your job

Wrzesniewski and her fellow researchers went on to interview people in many different roles, including engineers, nurses, and restaurant staff. In the resulting paper, "Crafting a Job: Revisioning Employees as Active Crafters of Their Work," they described how even people in highly prescribed jobs could make changes that would fundamentally alter their view of what they did:[10]

Job crafting changes the meaning of the work by changing job tasks or relationships in ways that allow employees to reframe the purpose of the job and experience the work differently. Psychological meaningfulness of work results when people feel worthwhile and valuable at work. Thus, any actions that employees take to alter their jobs in ways that increase feelings of purpose are likely to change the meaning of the work.

Specifically, Wrzesniewski noted that "job crafters" had changed three things about their work: the boundaries of their job (e.g., extra tasks they might do), how they related to others, and how they perceived the purpose of what they were doing. A nurse's handbook, for example, might have very specific guidelines for how to execute certain procedures. But some nurses in the study spent a bit more time informing and comforting the people they cared for. They interacted more with family members. They viewed themselves not as "just a nurse," but as patient advocates. Same hospital, same colleagues, but as a result of crafting their daily work, they were more likely to view what they did as more than "just a job."

The same held true for other professions. Computer engineers felt better when they offered help to colleagues. Short-order cooks felt better when they took extra steps to "create a product worthy of pride." While some people viewed their jobs as carrying out instructions, others proactively looked for ways to alter aspects of what they did, who they did it with, and how they viewed it.

Job crafting helped them tap into their own intrinsic motivators—control, competence, and connection—and they felt better about work.

In addition to them feeling better, their work was better. The researchers surveyed co-workers and managers of job crafters to ask about performance. (It was a blind test, so those being surveyed were not aware of who was job crafting and who wasn't.) The results showed that the colleagues of job crafters thought they were happier and performed better.

You can craft almost any kind of job. Sabine from the previous chapter, for example, started her experiments while she was still in the HR department at Siemens. Anja made efforts to use new technologies and share what she learned with her colleagues while she was a secretary. Mara used her job as a laboratory, experimenting with ways to develop new skills, then leveraged those skills to change roles in her company. These were all small steps that didn't require permission from someone else. (Wrzesniewski writes, "Perhaps job crafting's best feature is that it's driven by you, not your supervisor.") Yet those small steps had an impact on who they interacted with and how they viewed their work.

These are all examples of what Deci and Ryan meant by "self-determination." No matter what your current role is, you can start where you are, making small adjustments that help you tap into your drive and have a better experience at work.

Strategy #2: Discover more opportunities by building your network

But what if you're really in the wrong job, or just curious about whether other jobs might be better for you? Although you might be able to tap into your drive in poor conditions, it's certainly easier to do so in some environments than in others. For example, some jobs might have more opportunities for learning, or some companies might have a more nurturing, respectful culture. To increase your chances of moving to a better environment, you have to first discover those environments and then have some means of accessing them. The best way to do this is via other people.

More than thirty years before Facebook was launched, Mark Granovetter showed that having a larger, more diverse social network will improve your luck, increasing your knowledge about a broader set of possibilities and enhancing your ability to access them. In 1973, Granovetter analyzed the flow of information through social networks, and the resulting paper went on to become the most cited in all of social science. He called it "The Strength of Weak Ties" because the people we know well—our strong ties—tend to have the same information that we do. It's our weak ties that tend to have knowledge, connections, and other resources we might need to make some kind of change.

The example he used was finding jobs. Granovetter cited a range of studies showing that people find out about jobs through personal contacts more than by any other method. Then he conducted a study of his own and found that the information that led to people finding new jobs came via people they barely knew or via the contacts of those people. Though close friends and family might be more motivated to help you find a job, being able to access different information from weak ties was much more important. He noted how luck played a role in interacting with weak ties:[11]

Chance meetings or mutual friends operated to reactivate such ties. It is remarkable that people receive crucial information from individuals whose very existence they have forgotten.

The practical implications of this became clear to me at a networking event where I worked. Ten people were seated at a round banquet table, answering the question "How did you get your current job?" Our career paths all seemed like random walks. One recent graduate happened to attend our company's event on campus and wound up in an arcane business area she had never heard of before. Another person's company was acquired and, as a result, she now had a new boss and a new organizational culture. My favorite was an experienced person whose prior business was shut down. He got his current job after bumping into an old acquaintance at a bar. "I sent him a note, and here I am!"

I was no different. My career wasn't the result of a purposeful exploration of what might tap into my intrinsic needs and make the most of my potential. It was more like a series of accidents and coincidences, reactions to organizational changes and the decisions of other people. All of us at that networking event were playing career roulette, hoping we would land in a good environment, sometimes literally just waiting for a better opportunity to come along.

What Granovetter showed is that, by cultivating relationships and building a certain kind of network, you could increase your odds of coming into contact with more opportunities.

Making your own luck

Should you craft your job, or should you try to build relationships so you can explore other possibilities? The answer, as you might have guessed, is both. The people you'll meet throughout this book used the five elements of Working Out Loud to change their everyday experience while *also* developing relationships that expanded their sense of what was possible for them. WOL helped them take a more active role in shaping their future.

Results vary, of course. Some enjoy meeting more people. Some feel more curious and confident. Many more improve their skills and visibility, creating new opportunities at work and making it possible to discover new and rewarding roles. Once people experience self-determination, tapping into feelings of greater control, confidence, and connectedness, it's difficult to return to their old approach. "I could never go back," they tell me.

Don't wait for Fortune to smile upon you. With the right kind of effort, you can increase your access to people, knowledge, and other resources that can change both what you do and how you feel about what you do. Your destiny isn't something Fate hands to you, it can be something you create.

KEY IDEAS IN PART I

- We feel better when we tap into our drive—our innate psychological needs for control, competence, and connection.

- One strategy for tapping into your drive is to start where you are, crafting your current job by making adjustments to your tasks, relationships, and perceptions at work.

- To discover more opportunities, expand your network in a purposeful way. That earns you access to more knowledge, people, experiences, and possibilities.

- WOL is a way to implement your job crafting and network-building strategies. Doing so helps you tap into your innate psychological needs.

- Whatever your background, age, or social skills, you can learn to Work Out Loud.

PART II

The Five Elements of Working Out Loud

3

The Evolution of "Working Out Loud"

So, is it just blogging?

MY WIFE, AFTER ONE OF MY EARLY
ATTEMPTS AT DESCRIBING WOL

THERE ARE MANY, many things you can do "out loud." You can live, love, laugh, cry, dance, party, read, and think out loud, just to name a few.

The first reference I found to "working out loud" was in a short post by Glyn Moody from 2006, called "Thinking and Working Out Loud." It describes the author's reasons for blogging. "It's not enough to read all that's out there. I need to make sure I have digested, understood it and put it into context for myself... blogging has become my notebook and general repository of digital bits and bobs."[1]

Four years later, Bryce Williams offered a definition of "working out loud." He had been leading innovation and collaboration efforts at a large pharmaceutical company, and he used the phrase to describe "behaviors and critical outcomes of using Social Collaboration tools."[2] He provided a simple formula:

Working Out Loud =
Observable Work + Narrating Your Work

Williams wanted to encourage people to use social tools[3] to share their work, including finished products (such as presentations and other documents) as well as work in progress (what you're doing or learning, ideas you have). When I first saw the phrase, I thought the benefits of making your work visible would be clear. But when I talked to others about it, their reactions were decidedly mixed:

- *"Who cares what I'm working on?"*
- *"I don't have time for that."*
- *"Oh, I don't like to toot my own horn."*
- *"Why would I do that?"*

Even my wife struggled to understand the point of it. I tried to explain that making work visible was a means, not an end. Of course, just dumping things onto the internet or your company intranet isn't terribly useful. But the thoughtful sharing of your work can help others who are trying to do something similar. It can also help you get feedback and improve your work, and lead to new ideas and new connections.

Over coffee early one morning, after I had been writing *Working Out Loud* for several months, I proudly tried again to describe to my wife what it was all about. When I finished, there was an uncomfortable pause. "So," she said, "is it just blogging?"

I slumped my shoulders and sighed, like a slowly deflating balloon. "No," I said, "it's not just blogging." I went back to quietly sipping my coffee. I knew I had to come up with a better description of "working out loud," and better reasons why people should do it.

Making "Working Out Loud" mean much more

After that discussion with my wife, I kept experimenting with definitions: in presentations, in written material, in elevator conversations.

Working Out Loud is working in an open, generous, connected way that enables you to build a purposeful social network, become more effective, and access more opportunities.

Working Out Loud starts with making your work visible in such a way that it might help others. When you do that— when you work in a more open, connected way—you can build a purposeful network that makes you more effective and provides access to more opportunities.

These were better, but saying that Working Out Loud "starts with making your work visible" still felt limiting.

No megaphones, please

An email exchange with one of the first members of a WOL Circle helped me see things differently. She wrote to tell me she enjoyed her Circle and found it useful, but that she didn't want to be visible. I was confused. Why did she join a Circle then?

What made me join? Wanting to be connected and feeling somewhat emotionally unconnected to work. My team is great, and I really love being here, but the work itself is fairly dry and, dare I say it, uninspiring. So I guess I wanted a bit of a shake-up to see if I could feel more engaged about work (and life in general because work is a very large part of my life).

I'll add one more bit—while my goal itself has been deliberately not work related (I had been working for three years to get to VP and felt it was emotionally draining!), thinking about people and networks and just simple possibilities in a different way is already making me more open at and about work. I'm meeting more interesting people, and I am comfortable with the thought that the job need not be everything in life and that it is very easy to give back if I just look around.

When people first hear about Working Out Loud, they tend to focus on the "out loud" part. It's common to see megaphones on slides and articles about WOL, and there's often an emphasis on social media. But that's just a small part of what Working Out Loud has become. The way the early Circle member above described what she was looking for, and the benefits she experienced —"wanting to feel connected" and "making me more open"—made me see that WOL could be about much more than tools and sharing your work. As she experienced, it can change how you feel about yourself and others, and how you feel about the work you do.

WOL: A method and a mindset

After my failed attempts to convince people with descriptions of Working Out Loud, I decided to try to help them directly, so they could learn by doing and experience the benefits for themselves. I posted an offer on my company intranet to coach people one-on-one, and volunteers from a few different cities started to sign up.

We scheduled weekly phone calls, and I began by asking them about what they wanted to do or learn, or about a topic they wanted to explore. Then we would start listing people related to what they chose. We usually knew a few people we could add to the list, and we searched the company intranet and the internet for more. Over the coming weeks, we would try to build relationships with some of them based on generosity, as Keith Ferrazzi had taught me. Week after week we practiced offering a wide array of contributions in different ways.

It worked. People were shocked at their ability to connect with anyone, anywhere, and then deepen some of those relationships. They quickly saw how their expanded network gave them a greater sense of control while improving the odds of reaching their goal. Unlike with their previous networking experiences, they felt good about what they were doing because their efforts were authentic and focused on contribution.

Soon I started publishing the steps we took in our coaching sessions so people could practice WOL on their own, and that turned into the WOL Circle Guides, which matured over several years into a method that has spread to over sixty countries. More than a set of techniques, the guides capture an approach for relating to other people, to yourself, and to the work you do. What had begun as a phrase for sharing work on collaboration platforms had evolved to stand for something more—a mindset composed of five elements:

- Purposeful Discovery
- Relationships
- Generosity
- Visible Work
- A Growth Mindset

As for the description of Working Out Loud, there's still no single best elevator pitch, as I tend to describe WOL in different ways, depending on the audience and context. In a recent short video called "What Is Working Out Loud?" I describe it this way:[4]

Working Out Loud is a method for building relationships that can help you in some way, like achieving a goal, or developing a skill, exploring a new topic, or the next step in your career.

It's networking, but with a human twist.

Instead of networking to get something, Working Out Loud is about you making contributions to other people related to what you want to do. Those contributions can span a wide range, from offering attention and appreciation to sharing your work and experiences that might be helpful to other people.

It's not fake. It's not manipulative. You don't keep score or expect anything in return. But over time, your contributions build trust and deepen a sense of relatedness with other people, and that's what increases the chances for information exchange and collaboration with some of them.

In the rest of Part II, you'll learn about research on the five elements and how to apply them in practical ways. You'll read stories of people who embody them when they Work Out Loud. In Part III, you'll go through the steps of the Circle method for yourself.

KEY IDEAS IN THIS CHAPTER

- The definition of the phrase "working out loud" was originally limited to making your work visible on social tools, but has evolved to describe a method and a mindset.

- As a mindset, WOL has five elements: Purposeful Discovery, Relationships, Generosity, Visible Work, and a Growth Mindset.

- The five elements are interrelated, and people tend to emphasize different elements, depending on their attitudes and aptitudes. Combined, the elements create an open, generous, and connected approach to work and life.

- WOL Circles are a peer support method for putting the elements into practice so you can build your network and experience the benefits for yourself.

EXERCISES

Does anyone actually do the exercises in books? I didn't use to. But then I read *Steering by Starlight* by Martha Beck, and the exercises were so simple that I completed most of them by writing directly in the spaces provided. In this book I tried to emulate the simplicity and practicality of Martha Beck's exercises.

The remaining chapters each end with two exercises: something you can do in one minute and something you can do in five minutes. They're meant to be so quick and easy that you can do them on your phone, wherever you happen to be. Here are the first two:

Something you can do in less than a minute

Research cited in Part I shows how people in different roles are evenly split in viewing their work as a job, career, or calling. How do you view your work? Why?

Something you can do in less than 5 minutes

How did you get the job you have now? Is what you do for a living something you chose carefully after the purposeful exploration of a diverse set of alternatives? Or were you playing career roulette, leaving it to chance and hoping to land in a good spot?

4

Purposeful Discovery

"Follow your passion" might just be terrible advice.

CAL NEWPORT,
So Good They Can't Ignore You

THERE ARE MANY possible careers in the world and an infinite number of paths through life. How do you know which ones would be best for you? Where do you start looking?

At different stages in my life, I was sure I had the answer to the question "What should I do with my life?" When I was five, I was going to be a paleontologist, digging up dinosaur bones. At eleven I knew I would be a baseball player. As I grew older, my equally clear purposes in life were to be a psychologist, a reengineering consultant, and a computer scientist who would model how the brain works. None of that happened. Instead I spent more than twenty years working in big banks.

The sad part isn't that I didn't fulfill my early career aspirations. It's that I bought into a romantic myth of having One Special Purpose that I was never able to find or fulfill. In Alain de Botton's *The Pleasures and Sorrows of Work*, a career counselor describes the consequences of this common misconception:[1]

He remarked that the most common and unhelpful illusion plaguing those who came to see him was the idea that they ought somehow, in the normal course of events, to have intuited—long before they had finished their degrees, started families, bought houses, and risen to the top of law firms—what they should properly be doing with their lives. They were tormented by a residual notion of having through some error or stupidity on their part missed out on their true "calling."

One of the major problems with identifying your true calling is that you're aware of only a tiny fraction of the possibilities, and picking solely from what you already know is grossly limiting. Even if you can identify your passion and are willing to follow it, you can't know all of the different ways to turn that passion into a career, nor what that career will feel like once you do. Jordi Muñoz, for example, may have dreamed of being a pilot when he was four, but that's only because he had no idea about all the other kinds of jobs that might be better. When he was a teenager, the company he would ultimately work for and the technology it was based on didn't even exist.

At times I hoped that my path would simply manifest itself. Like the man who found his next job via a chance meeting in a bar, I relied on serendipity, those wonderful moments when things happen by chance in a beneficial way, to show me my next step. But the problem with relying on serendipity is that it is, by definition, unreliable. It leaves your happiness completely up to chance.

Fortunately, I found there's a much better way to guide your decision making that will lead you to more rewarding possibilities: Purposeful Discovery, a form of goal-oriented exploration.

Reasons to start small and adapt as you learn

Matt worked in the IT department of a big financial services firm, and he wanted a change. After considering it for some time, his idea was to combine his analytical skills with his finance experience and become a financial advisor. That seemed reasonable enough.

The first thing Matt thought to do was to get the necessary certification. Unfortunately, that required passing a demanding exam, which meant a lot of study time and a fair amount of money. When he asked his manager if the company would pay for preparation classes and the exam fee, his request was denied. Even though there were many jobs in the bank that required the certification, none were in the IT department where Matt and his manager worked. Matt was stuck. He saw this as a barrier he didn't know how to get past and was upset the company wasn't willing to invest in him. A year later, he still hadn't made any progress toward changing his job.

In *Designing Your Life*,[2] Bill Burnett and Dave Evans tell the story of Elise, who, like Sabine from chapter 1, was ready for something different after a long career in Human Resources. She knew exactly what it would be: an Italian deli that served "wonderful coffee and authentic Tuscan food." Elise had visited Tuscany and loved the cafés there, and she dreamed of creating something just like it.

She had saved enough to get started, collected all the recipes she needed, researched the best place near her home to locate such a business, and did it. She rented a place, totally renovated it, stocked it with the best products, and opened to great fanfare. It was an immense amount of work, and it was a roaring success. Everyone loved it. She was busier than ever. And in no time she was miserable.

Elise liked the *idea* of an Italian deli and café, but she never imagined the problems with hiring staff, managing inventory, and maintaining the store. She didn't know what she didn't know, and she didn't know how to find out.

A different approach to designing your life

University professors see this kind of thing happen all the time as their students feel forced to make big decisions regarding careers they barely know about. Become a doctor or lawyer? Join a consulting firm, a bank, or a start-up? In addition to not knowing much about what these careers might actually be like, students tend to have little insight into what else might be possible for them. How could they?

That's how Burnett and Evans came to write *Designing Your Life*. Dave Evans was a professor at the University of California, Berkeley, teaching "How to Find Your Vocation," and Bill Burnett was the head of the Design Program at Stanford University. They combined their interests and experience to use design thinking— "a method for practical, creative resolution of problems and creation of solutions"—to help students design their lives after university. (They have since certified Life Design Coaches around the world.)

To help people avoid making costly career mistakes, the authors advocate trying small experiments that allow you to learn more about the direction you want to go in before you spend a lot of time and money getting there. In their book, they call the approach "wayfinding":

Since there's no one destination in life, you can't put your goal into your GPS and get the turn-by-turn directions for how to get there. What you can do is pay attention to the clues in front of you, and make your best way forward with the tools you have at hand.

Burnett and Evans call these experiments "prototypes." Usually the term is reserved for an early implementation of a product or service, but it can also apply to jobs and careers. "The simplest and easiest form of prototyping," they write, "is a conversation":

You want to talk to someone who is either doing and living what you're contemplating, or has real experience and expertise in an area about which you have questions.

By sticking with a big first step, Matt spent a frustrating year waiting for permission, missing an opportunity to learn more about his potential new field and discover other possibilities. Elise took a big risk and a big leap only to find out she didn't like where she wound up. They both would have fared better had they searched for people related to their goals and had more conversations. *What do financial advisors do all day? What's the worst part about running a restaurant? Are there other kinds of jobs related to my interests?*

The Purposeful Discovery element builds on the idea of conversations as prototypes and expands the set of experiments you can do. Jordi Muñoz from chapter 1, for example, used contributions in an online community to discover ways to improve his skills and apply them in a wider range of contexts, including at a job he could never have imagined otherwise. Sabine, Anja, Mara, and I did our own kinds of experiments to help us find people related to our interests and find our way. With each step—contributions, connections, conversations —we learned more about what we liked and didn't like, discovered new people and new possibilities, and refined our goals as we explored further.

Joyce reinvents her career

A practical example of Purposeful Discovery is how Joyce explored new kinds of work late in her career. For more than twenty years, Joyce worked in New York City, managing complex global projects for several big banks. At times it was challenging, even exciting, and was well paid. But as the banking industry changed, so did the work, and so did Joyce. When her firm downsized, Joyce was faced with the daunting prospect of finding work in tough economic times.

When I met Joyce, it struck me how she was interested in always learning about the next new thing. One of those things was social media, back when Facebook and LinkedIn were just launched, and she started experimenting with them well before they became popular. Joyce would search out entrepreneurs and social media experts who could help her learn. To practice using social media for work, she volunteered to serve as the chief digital strategist of the Financial Women's Association of New York, where she was already a member. It was an unpaid role, but it allowed her to apply some of her learning in a business context. The role also helped her leverage an existing network to establish more meaningful connections and to present at conferences about social media.

At each event she would learn new things, make more connections, and further shape her reputation. Gradually, Joyce was no longer a former banker interested in social media, but instead a social media professional who happened to be a former banker.

While she was learning, she was helping. She would teach finance professionals about LinkedIn, organize her own networking events, and leverage her growing set of relationships by connecting people who could help each other. All of this learning and all of these connections opened up new possibilities. One of the highlights was Joyce appearing with Maria Bartiromo on CNBC, "offering advice for baby boomers suddenly back at the drawing board."

Over time, she combined her different skills and interests and started her own consulting firm, SocMediaFin, offering "social media strategy development and implementation for financial services and other highly regulated industries." She became a popular speaker at conferences and companies around the country, getting fulfillment from the daily interaction with her large, diverse, and still-growing network. That activity made it possible for her to teach a class on social media at CUNY's Baruch College and manage professional services for a software company specializing in social media for financial firms. A few years later, the different elements of her career—working in big companies, making several career transitions, her ability to develop new skills and shape her reputation—made her an excellent choice to help others do the same. So, a global outplacement firm approached Joyce to lead their New York office.

Joyce could have easily dismissed her early interest in social media as a hobby, or told herself, "I'm not good enough." After all, there were plenty of other people who were younger and had more experience. But she kept trying new things, making connections, and learning along the way. Instead of starting with one fixed destination in mind and planning the steps to get there, Joyce began with interests and experiments which, over time, led her to some unexpected and wonderful places. Instead of facing a dwindling set of prospects after leaving the project management role at a big bank, Joyce now has more options than ever.

Brandon turns his hobby into a mission

What if you don't have a clear career direction in mind? The story of Brandon Stanton, creator of Humans of New York, shows how even a vague idea, when combined with the other elements of WOL, can orient your activities and help you discover possibilities you might never have considered.

Brandon grew up in a suburb of Atlanta, studied history at the University of Georgia, and took his first job as a bond trader in Chicago. A few years later, in the aftermath of the financial crisis, he was laid off. Without much money and with few prospects of getting another financial job at the time, Brandon decided to try something different. He had recently purchased a nice camera and enjoyed taking photos while walking around Chicago, so he decided his goal would be to practice his hobby as he traveled around the United States. Like many thousands of people interested in photography, Brandon's first idea was to create a photo blog based on his travels in different cities:[3]

My first stop was New Orleans, then Pittsburgh, then Philadelphia. Each time I arrived in a new city, I'd get lost in the streets and photograph everything that looked interesting, taking nearly a thousand photographs every day. After each day of shooting, I'd select thirty or forty of my favorite photographs and post them on Facebook. I named the albums after my first impression of each city. Pittsburgh was Yellow Steel Bridges. Philadelphia was Bricks and Flags. I had no big ambitions at the time. All I had was some vague, naive idea of making a living by selling prints of my best photos. In the meantime, I was just posting them for my family and friends to enjoy.

He had other ideas too, including plotting street portraits on an interactive map to create a photographic census of the city. But it was only through actually doing the work, posting it publicly on Facebook and getting feedback, that he started to try other things. Along with the usual city scenes, he started taking candid street portraits. When those portraits received a favorable response, he started asking his subjects questions and including snippets of the interview with each photo.

By the time he arrived in New York, almost all of his photographs were of people. He decided to give his new Facebook albums the now-famous name "Humans of New York." He never intended to stay, but by the end of the summer, after a short trip to Chicago to collect his things, he moved back to New York for good.

Brandon's goal kept evolving. Without any formal training in photography, he gradually kept learning to take better photos and get better results when approaching people. ("At first, the rejections sting," he said.[4]) In less than two years, what started as simple online photo albums had attracted thirty thousand likes, then sixty thousand, and soon other people started to copy his work, creating Humans of Copenhagen, Humans of Tel Aviv, and more. Such groups helped to further spread the word about Brandon and his work. A year later, his number of Facebook fans had skyrocketed to over a million. Brandon was still shooting photos, but other things became possible, including the launch of a book, an "inspiring collection of photographs and stories capturing the spirit of a city," that became a number-one *New York Times* best seller. He was named one of *Time* magazine's "30 Under 30," attracting yet more attention and opening up more possibilities. Brandon reflected on how he was able to change his life in a way that was not possible before:[5]

Humans of New York is an amazing story, and it's a story that could not have happened ten years ago. Without social media, I'd probably just be a quirky amateur photographer with a hard drive full of photos. I'd be cold-calling respected publications, begging for a feature. I may have even quit by now. Instead, I've discovered a daily audience of nearly a million people. Or should I say they discovered me.

With the success he was experiencing, Brandon's goal shifted again. He was starting to make money and decided early on to give some of it away, to try to do more with his photos than he had considered possible before. He described it in an online interview:[6]

I don't want to "cash out" or "monetize" HONY [Humans of New York]. I like to say it publicly because I want my audience to keep me on mission. HONY print sales have raised nearly $500,000 for charity in the past six months. I want to further monetize the site for nonprofit ventures. I honestly want to "give" HONY to New York in some way.

Brandon's Facebook page has more than eighteen million followers, and there are millions of followers on other platforms too. He published more best sellers. He went on a fifty-day world tour of twelve countries sponsored by the United Nations that included Iran, Iraq, Ukraine, Kenya, and South Sudan. Why go to these places? "The work has a very humanizing effect in places that are misunderstood or feared," he said. His purpose had shifted yet again, and his fans noticed it, as expressed in a comment on a photo of four women in Iraq: "You are changing the world one interview at a time. I am very grateful."[7]

Brandon's story combines all five elements of WOL. He made his work visible, and the feedback helped him get better while also helping him develop connections that could benefit him. He was generous with his work, posting it freely, and also generous with the eventual proceeds from that work. Importantly, he used his initial goal as a step toward exploring a range of possibilities that might be more meaningful and fulfilling. As a result of that exploration, in just over three years, he fundamentally changed his career and life—from out-of-work bond trader to beloved photographer, author, and philanthropist.

Finding your own way

Many of us were raised in an era when it was difficult and expensive to build things, and the cost of mistakes was high. You might get just one chance to plan, implement, and ship a product or service. As a result, you needed to put most of your effort into planning so you could ensure the product was right the first time. One of the many problems with this model was that you didn't know what "right" meant until other people gave you feedback after seeing or using whatever you built. Creating things was thus a risky proposition, reserved for institutions that could afford a big investment in planning and the occasional costly mistake.

The same used to be true for careers. You had to decide what you wanted to do for a living early on, typically well before you knew whether your choice was a good one for you. You planned as best you could, but once you fell into a certain track it was too expensive or difficult to try something else.

Reid Hoffman, the co-founder of LinkedIn, suggests we can now take a different approach to developing our career. In *The Start-up of You*, he says, "if you want to seize the new opportunities and meet the challenges of today's fractured career landscape, you need to think and act like you're running a start-up: your career."[8]

Why? Start-ups—and the entrepreneurs who run them—are nimble. They invest in themselves. They build their professional networks. They take intelligent risks. They make uncertainty and volatility work to their advantage. These are the very same skills professionals need to get ahead today . . .

The career landscape isn't what it used to be. Conventional career planning can work under certain conditions of relative stability, but in times of uncertainty and rapid change, it is severely limiting, if not dangerous. You will change. The environment around you will change.

Today, start-ups embrace an entirely different model for developing products and services. It's called "lean start-up," and it aims to get feedback at the very beginning of the process, not the end.[9] Whatever product or service an entrepreneur has in mind, they first create a minimum viable product—something that communicates the core idea but uses the fewest resources possible—and get that in front of potential users or customers. Because producing things has become so much simpler and cheaper, modern entrepreneurs spend less time on abstract planning and much more time creating and getting feedback. Instead of one cycle for planning and implementation, they keep iterating, getting more feedback, and making adjustments each time to improve things.

Purposeful Discovery is the equivalent of lean start-up for your own career and life. It's the approach that made it possible for Joyce and Brandon to find work they were good at and cared about. Your initial goal orients your activities, including the prototypes or experiments you'll try, the conversations you'll have, and contributions you'll make that will enable you to get feedback and learn. Based on what you discover, you adapt your goal and conduct the next round of experiments. You won't do it alone, though. The next element, Relationships, will be a source of support for you as well as a wellspring of resources and opportunities that can help you.

KEY IDEAS IN THIS CHAPTER

- Picking a job or career solely from what you already know is grossly limiting.

- Purposeful Discovery is a form of goal-oriented exploration to guide your decision making and lead to better possibilities.

- Instead of big risks and big leaps towards a fixed destination, try small experiments or prototypes to learn more about a potential new job or direction and discover other possibilities.

- "The simplest and easiest form of prototyping is a conversation." Who's already doing what you would like to do? What are the best and worst parts about their experience? What else can you learn from them?

- You can think of Purposeful Discovery as the equivalent of lean start-up for you and your career. Like a start-up, your initial goal orients your activities. As you get feedback and learn, you adapt your goal accordingly.

EXERCISES

Something you can do in less than a minute

What sparks your interest and curiosity? What would you be interested in learning more about? Start a list and write down as many topics as come to mind within a minute. These can serve as the basis for your Purposeful Discovery and can be a source of inspiration for when you choose a goal in chapter 10.

Something you can do in less than 5 minutes

If you don't have a Twitter account, create a basic one now. You can pick a photo and add other details later.

If you already have an account, take a few minutes to review whom you're following. Is it purposeful? Does it help you discover and learn?

If you think you don't like Twitter, consider creating an account as an experiment instead of a commitment. Even if you never tweet yourself, having an account allows you to learn about and interact with a wider range of people than was ever possible before, and is a useful asset for Purposeful Discovery.

5

Relationships

*Social networks have value precisely
because they can help us to achieve what we
could not achieve on our own.*

**NICHOLAS CHRISTAKIS
AND JAMES FOWLER,** Connected

ARE YOU SOCIAL?

Before you respond too quickly, the answer is yes. Whether or not you tweet or enjoy dinner parties, you're wired as a human being to be social. In *Connected*, researchers Nicholas Christakis and James Fowler show how social influence extends to almost every part of our lives:[1]

Networks influence the spread of joy, the search for sexual partners, the maintenance of health, the functioning of markets, and the struggle for democracy. Yet,

69

social-network effects are not always positive. Depression, obesity, sexually transmitted diseases, financial panics, violence, and even suicide also spread. Social networks, it turns out, tend to magnify whatever they are seeded with.

The research confirms what we've known for a long time: your networks of relationships matter. They change who you are. A popular shorthand for this is that "you are the average of the five people you associate with most." That may be an oversimplification, but your parents were right to pay attention to who you spent time with.

Your networks also change what you can become. If developed properly, they give you access to knowledge, expertise, and influence, extending the perimeter of your potential. One of the many things that will traverse your social connections is your reputation—who you are, what you do, and how well you do it. As sociologist Mark Granovetter demonstrated in 1973 in his paper "The Strength of Weak Ties," the better your network, the better your odds. Ronald Burt, a sociologist and professor at the University of Chicago Booth School of Business, also showed how people with better networks receive higher performance ratings, get promoted faster, and earn more money.

Building a better network is why people join exclusive clubs, go to certain schools, and attend conferences. It's why Dale Carnegie's *How to Win Friends and Influence People* still sells so many copies. (When he first published it in 1936 as "a practical, working handbook on human relations," he printed five thousand copies. It went on to sell fifteen million and is still popular over eighty years later. "People are frequently astonished at the new results they achieve," he wrote. "It all seems like magic."[2]) It's why Relationships is one of the five elements of Working Out Loud.

What is a relationship?

Most of us have a narrow definition of "relationship." We think in terms of family and friends, maybe a few colleagues that we like. Anthropologist Robin Dunbar famously proposed that the "maximum network size . . . predicted for humans on the basis of the size of their neocortex" is 150,[3] and Dunbar's number is widely quoted as an upper limit of how many stable relationships we can maintain.

But that only applies to a certain kind of relationship: "people you would not feel embarrassed about joining uninvited for a drink if you happened to bump into them in a bar."[4] Christakis and Fowler showed that the networks that influence you (and that you influence) are much, much larger. Even if you don't know a person well, or how they relate to others in your network, you can feel a sense of relatedness with them, and *that* is what increases influence, trust, cooperation, and collaboration.

An unsettling ethics experiment called "The Trolley Problem" demonstrates the truth of this. Try it for yourself.

A runaway trolley is headed toward five people who are tied up on the track. You are standing next to a lever that controls a switch. If you pull the lever you will redirect the trolley onto a side track, where there is one person tied up. You must choose between two options:

1 *Do nothing, allowing the trolley to hit and kill five people on the main track.*
2 *Take action and pull the lever, sending the trolley down the side track and causing the death of one person.*

What do you do?

In *Behave: The Biology of Humans at Our Best and Worst*, Robert Sapolsky describes experiments involving variations of this problem. What if that one person on the side track was your brother, or went to your high school, or was wearing the jersey of your favorite team? Would you kill five strangers to save one person you felt connected to in some way? Absolutely. One experiment involved making a choice between saving either a human being or a dog that was in front of a bus hurtling toward them. "Remarkably, 46% of women would save their dog over a foreign tourist if both were menaced by a runaway bus."[5]

The evolutionary explanation is that they feel more kinship with the dog. We have evolved to quickly identify who is like us and who isn't. Even infants are programmed to do it. Over many millennia, the ability to discriminate helped biologically related members pass on their genes, since the forces of group-level natural selection led to prosocial behaviors within a group and competition between groups. But Sapolsky notes that our sense of kinship goes far beyond genetics: "We treat people like relatives when they *feel* like relatives." The women helped their dog not because of their genes but because of a feeling, a sense of relatedness. That is something we can cultivate, and, depending on how we do so, it can have either positive or negative effects.

Relationships at work

One unfortunate consequence of our primal need to identify with our group is that employees in an organization quickly do so within different divisions, locations, and teams. As a result, no matter where you work, there is an Us and a Them wherever you look, with everyone lamenting the "silo mentality" while management exhorts people to collaborate more.

A group from Carnegie Mellon and SUNY Stony Brook set out to learn what it is that makes people more willing to cooperate and collaborate. They examined information exchanges between researchers at Bell Labs, and the contributions they made to each other's work, including authoring papers together. The results probably won't surprise you.

The best predictor was... the distance between their offices. Scientists who worked next to each other were 3 times more likely to discuss technical topics that led to collaboration than scientists who sat 30 feet from one another. Put them 90 feet apart, and they are as likely to collaborate as those who work several miles away! The probability of collaboration sharply decreases in a matter of a few feet.[6]

The interesting part, though, is *why* physical distance matters so much.

Observational and survey studies of work teams have suggested that two important mechanisms by which proximity promotes collaborative work are through support for passive awareness of others' activities and by the facilitation of informal communication. When people are co-located, they can view others' activities and overhear others' discussions, thereby learning about the existence of new potential collaborators and monitoring the progress of their current collaborators. Proximity also facilitates informal conversations, which can serve to enhance social relationships and work coordination.[7]

In short, the researchers found that, over time, informal conversations and awareness of what another person is doing (*"What are you up to?" "How's your project going?" "Any plans this weekend?"*) lead to a feeling of propinquity, a nice word that describes both the state of being close to someone and also kinship, a feeling of relatedness. A greater feeling of relatedness, they found, increases the chances for information exchange, cooperation, and collaboration.

This feeling is the essence of the Relationships element in WOL, and it's a feeling you can cultivate in a way that's simple, authentic, and positive.

Networking, with a human twist

"Networking" is the traditional corporate device for developing propinquity. Unfortunately, it was never an activity I associated with feeling close to another person. For me, networking meant shallow small talk and the exchange of business cards. It felt fake and manipulative. Although I enjoy talking with people, I always felt uncomfortable "networking" with them. As a result, for most of my career I had few meaningful relationships outside of family, friends, and the people I happened to be working with.

It wasn't until I was in my mid-forties that I started to understand what networking could be. What completely changed my approach to networking and to relationships in general was the Keith Ferrazzi Relationship Masters Academy course that I mentioned in the introduction. Looking back, I'm still struck by my good fortune to participate in it. I had just read Ferrazzi's *Never Eat Alone*, and he was giving a talk at my firm as part of a tour promoting his new book, *Who's Got Your Back*. Hundreds of people crammed into the room to hear him speak, and at the end, almost as an afterthought, he mentioned a year-long course he was piloting and offered four spots to people at our firm. That evening I wrote a note to the head of Human Resources to make a case for taking one of those spots, and I got in.

In the course, we learned techniques for reaching more people and expanding our network. More importantly, we discussed four mindsets that serve as "the behavioral foundation" of developing richer and more meaningful relationships. According to Ferrazzi, these are:[8]

Generosity: The willingness to offer something of yourself without expecting something in return.

Vulnerability: When you admit to a failing or weakness, you demonstrate trust in other people and make it easier for them to be authentic.

Candor: Being direct and honest with others shows you value them more than you value anything you might get from them.

Accountability: Doing what you say you will do—and admitting when you haven't—is another way to build trust.

Put together, these mindsets lead to greater intimacy, enabling people to get to know and care about each other. I remember my cynicism when we started talking about it. Intimacy and networking? But throughout the course, we practiced applying these concepts as we worked with each other in class, and as we reached out to others outside of the course. When it came to intimacy, for example, there was an exercise in which we sat next to people we didn't know over dinner and had "forty-five minutes to care about them." We turned to each other with a look of dread and anxiety. But we did it, and ten years later I still remember the dinner that night, and the person with whom I talked. As Ferrazzi said during the class, "When you know someone, really get to know them as a human being, how could you not care?"

At work and at home, I started to replace small talk with conversations that showed my genuine interest in the other person. I asked more questions and became a better listener. I was humbler and more vulnerable. The results, just as Dale Carnegie wrote in 1936, seemed like magic. Instead of feeling shallow and manipulative, networking now felt authentic and helpful. I saw that making connections wasn't about collecting contacts but about building deeper, more meaningful relationships with people.

But what if you could have this kind of connection with almost anyone? What if a feeling of relatedness wasn't limited to people you meet in person?

Digital propinquity

In the time since that study of researchers at Bell Labs (which identified that "passive awareness of others' activities" and "informal communication" increased the chances for collaboration), social technologies have come along that enable that kind of communication with people across geographies and time zones. In a *New York Times Magazine* article titled "Brave New World of Digital Intimacy," Clive Thompson describes the sense of relatedness, or "ambient awareness," that comes from the short updates and activity streams in most social platforms:[9]

It is, they say, very much like being physically near someone and picking up on his mood through the little things he does—body language, sighs, stray comments—out of the corner of your eye ... This is the paradox of ambient awareness. Each little update—each individual bit of social information—is insignificant on its own, even supremely mundane. But taken together, over time, the little snippets coalesce into a surprisingly sophisticated portrait of your friends' and family members' lives, like thousands of dots making a pointillist painting. This was never before possible ...

This isn't to suggest that online connections replace the need for in-person interactions, or that they're equivalent. But it does mean that, when used purposefully and intentionally (as described in the following chapters), modern tools can help you develop a sense of relatedness with a larger, more diverse group of people than you may have thought possible.

Some networks are better than others

The authors of *Connected* show that, yes, networks are key to transmission: of information, practices, and even unwanted things like diseases. But they also show that the *kind* of network matters, depending on what is being transmitted. For example, certain types of information will pass only between people who trust each other. Diseases, in contrast, can become epidemics if they are passed to connections outside of the initial group—say, an infected person who gets on a plane to a foreign country.

Over the last century, mathematicians have become increasingly interested in studying different kinds of networks, trying to come up with models that emulate our experiences with networks in the real world, including social networks. The model would have to explain how, for example, most people have a relatively small set of connections, yet in study after study there seem to be only six or so degrees of separation between any two people. How and why is that possible?

In 1998, Duncan Watts and Steven Strogatz came up with an explanation. In a short, dense paper titled "Collective Dynamics of 'Small-World' Networks," they show how a certain kind of network would be effective at transmitting messages while also emulating our experience in real life.[10] Underlying the rigorous mathematics, a small-world network has two simple characteristics. The first is that such a network includes small clusters that are densely connected. Think of a group of five people where everyone is connected to everyone else. The second characteristic of small-world networks is that larger groups are sparsely connected. Think of two clusters, for example, with only one person in common. Researchers have discovered small-world network properties in real-world phenomena ranging from electric power grids to neural networks to social networks. Why? It seems that all kinds of systems are trying to optimize the efficiency of different networks, balancing the benefits of being connected with the costs of maintaining those connections.

In a group of twenty-five people, for example, the most robust network might be to have everyone know everyone else, but that would require three hundred connections. You could get most of the networking benefits with a fifth of those connections by forming five densely connected groups (ten connections each) and having a few people who are members of multiple groups.

As you build your social network, you're not trying to maximize your number of connections or even your number of deep relationships. You're trying to build a network with both strong and weak ties. You need clusters of connections who trust you so you can exchange sensitive and valuable information. You also need people who are different from you—in geography, jobs, and interests—because they'll have information and contacts you and your strong ties don't have.

If all of this sounds a bit technical, it might help you to think of an online group or another community of which you're a member, perhaps related to a hobby or topic you care about. A *Harvard Business Review* article titled "How to Build Your Network" notes that "shared activities bring together a cross-section of disparate individuals around a common point of interest, instead of connecting similar individuals with shared backgrounds."[11] Such a group can be a good example of a small-world network, since it tends to have a diverse mix of strong and weak ties. You may have a few friends in the group, and most other people will be different in terms of age, location, knowledge, and other attributes.

How and why Nikolay builds his network

Nikolay is an engineer in Moscow who specializes in improving the performance of databases, and he's extremely good at what he does. Yet, when he began his job, it quickly became clear that the only people who would ever be aware of Nikolay or his work would be his manager and the few people who had to call on him for help. He set out to change that—to have more people around the company and around the world know who he is and what he's capable of.

To start building his network, Nikolay joined an online community of four hundred database experts on his company's collaboration platform, and began regularly posting technical content there that might help other engineers (for example, "A handy utility for analyzing SQL plans"). He organized local meet-ups where others could contribute and learn from each other. He would actively search for people posting database problems so he could offer his assistance.

Four hundred people inside the large global company where we both worked may not seem like a lot. But they are the four hundred people in the firm who matter most to Nikolay, because they're precisely the people who have access to database jobs around the world. As a result of his contributions, anyone searching for "database performance" or "database community" would find Nikolay. Without even knowing his title or his manager, they would quickly see his work and realize that he is a leading expert in the company for the specific engineering topic they cared about. He would be an expert not just because he said so, but because his contributions were visible, and because others provided positive feedback on his work. Nikolay is applying this same approach externally, using a public blog at savvinov.com. There, he publishes insights into different aspects of his specialty, the performance tuning of Oracle databases. He even offers "free tuning help to beginners."

Through his contributions, both in person and online, more people know about Nikolay and his work. He has taken control of his reputation as an expert and increased his access to opportunities. His career no longer depends solely on his relationship with his manager in Moscow or on a one-page resume. Instead, his online body of work, the generous and consistent way in which it's offered, and the public feedback on his contributions are all increasing his access to new opportunities in case he ever wants to make a change.

Building your own best network

Even if we've known for a long time that relationships are important, social scientists are now able to analyze just how powerful they are. They understand what it takes to build a sense of relatedness that increases the chances of information exchange and collaboration. They also know the particular kinds of networks that are most helpful. This means it can be easier than ever for you to develop your own small-world network of relationships, a set of strong and weak ties that can help you in a wide range of ways.

The next element, Generosity, is what transforms networking from something that might feel inauthentic or uncomfortable into something you enjoy—a natural means of exploring and relating.

KEY IDEAS IN THIS CHAPTER

- Your network shapes both who you are and what you can become. If developed properly, it gives you access to knowledge, expertise, and influence.

- As social animals, we have evolved to quickly identify Us and Them—who we are related to. The Trolley Problem illustrates how this sense of kinship influences how we treat others.

- Importantly, the feeling of relatedness can be cultivated, leading to greater chances for information exchange, cooperation, and collaboration.

- Generosity, vulnerability, candor, accountability, and intimacy serve as the behavioral foundation for deepening your relationships, and they transform networking from something that might feel inauthentic to something that's fulfilling.

- A good network includes clusters of strong ties with people who trust you, so you can exchange valuable information, as well as weak ties with people who are different from you, who have information and contacts that you and your strong ties don't have.

EXERCISES

Something you can do in less than a minute

Reflect on the people you consider to be in your network. If you feel a sense of relatedness with some of them, how did you develop that feeling? Is it your experience that such a feeling can lead to greater trust, information exchange, and cooperation?

Something you can do in less than 5 minutes

Create a basic LinkedIn profile. (As with your Twitter account, you can pick a photo and add other details later.)

If you already have a profile, take a look at it now. Is it current? Is it the kind of profile you would like to see when you search for other people?

If you don't like the idea of using LinkedIn, think of it as a simple online business card, something that most people have and expect others to have.

6

Generosity

The world is full of people who are grabbing and self-seeking. So the rare individual who unselfishly tries to serve others has an enormous advantage. He has little competition.

DALE CARNEGIE,
How to Win Friends and Influence People

IMAGINE YOU'RE READING this book while lazing by the pool at a fancy resort. You're alone, sipping fresh coconut water straight from the coconut, when you hear a cry for help. You can see that a man is drowning, and you quickly calculate that there's a 50/50 chance the person will die if you don't help him, and a 5 percent chance you'll both drown if you attempt to rescue him. What would you do?

It turns out that we have evolved to want to save the other person. That's because, if we each choose to save the drowning man, and if others are likely to reciprocate (because we've evolved with similar instincts), then we all reduce our chances of drowning, and so will be more likely to pass on our genes.

The evolution of reciprocal altruism

The name for this behavior is "reciprocal altruism," and it isn't limited to humans. In 1937, Meredith Crawford put two young chimpanzees in a cage, and showed that they too are wired to help each other under certain conditions.[1] In the experiment, a heavy box with food on top was placed outside the cage. The chimps could pull on ropes connected to the box to bring it closer and get the food, but the box was too heavy for any one chimp to pull alone. To get the food, they had to cooperate. Fairly quickly, two hungry chimps learned to pull in unison so they could both get the food. Even more interesting, when only one of the chimps was hungry, the chimp that didn't want the food *pulled the box anyway*. Though the hungry one wound up eating everything, the other chimp helped in return for a greater chance of reciprocity in the future.

In 1971, Robert Trivers provided a comprehensive model for this behavior. In a fascinating paper titled "The Evolution of Reciprocal Altruism," he analyzes birds that cry out to warn of predators despite the threat of disclosing their own location.[2] He also describes in detail the behaviors of fish that groom other fish despite the threat of being eaten. Groupers, for example, are large predators with brains that are simple, relative to ours. They've evolved to take advantage of the long-term benefits of being serviced by parasite-eating cleaner fish while sacrificing the short-term benefit of an easy meal. Even after a cleaning, groupers won't eat the cleaner fish, to preserve the likelihood of future cleanings. While we may think of the world as being a dog-eat-dog competitive environment, it can also be "fish help other fish" and everybody wins.

Frans de Waal, a director at the Yerkes National Primate Research Center in Atlanta, studied capuchin monkeys to dig further into the conditions in which those animals cooperated, and with whom. He showed that, when given a choice, capuchins prefer helping themselves plus a partner over helping only themselves. In the paper he released with his fellow researchers, he calls this "prosocial behavior," and finds that subjects systematically favor the prosocial option if their partner is familiar, visible, and fair.[3]

We believe prosocial behavior is empathy based. Empathy increases in both humans and animals with social closeness, and in our study, closer partners made more prosocial choices.

The deeper the relationship with people in your network, the more likely they are to help you.

Combining the "two great forces of human nature"

Humans have an even greater capacity for the cognitive demands of reciprocal altruism. To use the earlier example, we have a greater ability to calculate the costs and benefits of saving a drowning person. Beyond this rational capacity, we experience emotional rewards that affect the kinds of help we offer, and emotional bonds that affect our choice of recipient for that help. Our system of giving and receiving is much more complicated than tit for tat. Adam Grant, a professor at the Wharton School, explores this in his book *Give and Take*. He shows how you can be both generous and purposeful:[4]

Most people assume that self-interest and other-interest are opposite ends of one continuum. Yet in my studies of what drives people at work, I've consistently found that self-interest and other-interest are completely independent motivations: you can have both of them at the same time. As Bill Gates argued at the World Economic Forum, "there are two great forces of human nature: self-interest, and caring for others," and people are most successful when they are driven by a "hybrid engine" of the two. If takers are selfish and failed givers are selfless, successful givers are otherish: they care about benefitting others, but they also have ambitious goals for advancing their own interests.

The giving and receiving are not limited to one-to-one transactions. There's no need to keep score. Rather, you offer genuine contributions without expectations to individuals in your network, and reciprocal altruism makes it likely that others in your network will respond. You give and you also benefit in a way that's normal and natural.

What do you have to offer?

The question "What do you have to offer?" seems to make even the most skilled and generous people uncomfortable. If you're saving someone who's drowning, or cleaning a grouper of ectoparasites, then it's clear what it means to help others. But applied to everyday life, the idea of serving others can seem too abstract or naive. As a result, many of us feel hesitant about giving others even the simplest things.

The severity of the problem became clear to me one day as I sat with a former high school classmate who was looking to change jobs. As we talked, I was struck by his deep understanding of the complex business he was in, how that work brought him into contact with many African countries, and his near encyclopedic knowledge of music. He's also married and has children, and we shared stories about our families. Talking with him was a pleasure. Yet he struggled with building his network. When I asked him about the contributions he could make to deepen relationships, he paused and looked embarrassed.

Despite all his skills and experiences, he simply didn't know what to offer other people or how to offer it.

You already have valuable gifts

When Dale Carnegie writes about the best approach to building relationships, he doesn't mention wealth or highly specialized skills. His advice includes things anyone can do:[5]

- *Give honest and sincere appreciation.*
- *Become genuinely interested in other people.*
- *Talk in terms of the other person's interests.*
- *Be a good listener.*
- *Encourage other people to talk about themselves.*
- *Make the other person feel important—and do it sincerely.*

Keith Ferrazzi calls these "universal currencies," things anyone can give and anyone would like to receive. They're simple yet powerful. Think of the last time someone gave you specific positive feedback about your work. How did that make you feel? Or when someone trusted you enough to be vulnerable. How often does that happen? Universal currencies can be among the most valuable gifts we have to offer.

With social tools, it has become easier than ever to offer these simple gifts in addition to what you might do in person. Here are just a few examples:

- Thank someone.
- Offer public, positive feedback on work you admire.
- Connect people for their mutual benefit.

You have so much to offer, and we haven't yet mentioned the many things specific to you—to your job, your education, your culture, your life experiences. This is just a start, and there will be a more complete guide to contributions in Part III, including when and how to offer them. For now, the point is for you to think broadly and in a human way about all that you have to offer. Nikolay offered his help to people in his community. Jordi contributed his designs. Anja and Sabine shared what they were learning at work. Brandon posted his photos. They all led with helpful, genuine contributions, and they all benefited as a result.

Here's an example of someone who freely shares his knowledge and experience every day. Though he's already successful and wealthy, his contributions help him reach more people and gain access to even more possibilities.

Fred Wilson, venture capitalist

When it comes to leading with generosity, venture capitalists might not come to mind. But Fred Wilson is not your average venture capitalist. He's the co-founder of Union Square Ventures, a New York City–based venture capital firm whose portfolio includes internet companies such as Twitter, Tumblr, Foursquare, Zynga, and Kickstarter. He also blogs every day.

He started when he was forty-two. During the last fifteen years, he's written over eight thousand posts on his website, avc.com, attracting close to ten million unique visitors. He writes mostly about technology and technology start-ups, offering insights that can help entrepreneurs and investors, as well as anyone interested in current business trends. One series, for example, is called "MBA Mondays" and provides detailed advice to entrepreneurs on everything from hiring to employee equity to how to scale a company. He also shares his personal experiences, from business failures to music he likes. As much as I enjoy these daily posts, Fred Wilson benefits too.[6]

I write every day. It is my discipline, my practice, my thing. It forces me to think, articulate, and question. And I get feedback from it. When I hit publish, I get a rush. Every time. Just like the first time. It is incredibly powerful.

Wilson's daily contributions also allow him to reach a much broader audience than he could otherwise, despite most venture capitalists having an excellent network. In addition to the millions of web visits, more than ten thousand people have contributed over 150,000 comments. The "AVC community," as Fred refers to them, has debated issues, pushed for legislation, and funded good causes. That community even led Fred to explore possibilities in an area quite different from the venture capital business: public school education.[7]

A number of years ago, I wrote a blog post talking about the need to teach middle school and high school students how to write software. In the comments (where the good stuff happens), a Google engineer told me to go down to Stuyvesant High School and meet a teacher named Mike Zamansky who had taught him to write code in high school. So I did that and thus begun my education into the world of computer science education in the NYC public high school system. What I learned was that other than Mike's program at Stuyvesant and a few other small programs, there wasn't much. So began my quest to see more computer science and software engineering in the NYC public school system.

Wilson went on to provide the initial funding for what became the first Academy for Software Engineering in downtown New York City, and he's an increasingly vocal, visible advocate for education.

Giving as a way to make work and life better

Another venture capitalist who shares the perspective of Fred Wilson is Reid Hoffman. In an insightful article titled "Connections with Integrity," he describes why leading with generosity is important:[8]

I believe that the people who tend to become more effective in the world are those who build and nurture the best alliances.

One way to help nurture good alliances is to provide early and explicit signs of your own commitment, showing people that you actually care about helping them. My name for this practice is the "theory of small gifts." There are many small ways to invest in a relationship and create more value for everyone, without expecting anything tangible in return. For example, you can offer to introduce people to others in your network; if the introduction is well chosen, it can be one of the most valuable things you can do for someone . . .

It seems counterintuitive, but the more altruistic your attitude, the more benefits you will gain from the relationship. If you insist on a quid pro quo every time you help others, you will have a much narrower network and a more limited set of opportunities. Conversely, if you set out to help others . . . simply because you think it's the right thing to do, you will rapidly reinforce your own reputation and expand your universe of possibilities.

Fred Wilson, Reid Hoffman, Keith Ferrazzi, and Dale Carnegie aren't pure altruists. They have all run successful businesses, fully aware that they have a limited amount of resources to share. But like all of the different species that practice reciprocal altruism, they understand that certain gifts, freely given, increase their own long-term chances for success. That's why Generosity is an element of Working Out Loud, and why Keith Ferrazzi says "the currency of real networking is not greed but generosity."[9]

You won't know which individuals in your network will help you in the future, so you lead with generosity and empathy in all of your interactions. The next element, Visible Work, will further expand the set of contributions you can make and show how you can make them.

KEY IDEAS IN THIS CHAPTER

- Self-interest and other-interest are completely independent motivations: you can have both of them at the same time.

- You already have the most valuable gifts there are to offer.

- Even Fred Wilson, a wealthy and successful venture capitalist, finds he can build a more diverse network and access more possibilities through a range of small gifts, freely given.

- It seems counterintuitive, but the more altruistic your attitude, the more benefits you will gain from the relationship.

EXERCISES

Something you can do in less than a minute

Post this on Twitter or LinkedIn: "Reading *Working Out Loud* by @johnstepper"

This is an example of offering attention. (Thank you very much.) If you @-mention me, I'll be alerted and will respond, showing you how even a simple six-word contribution can create a connection that wouldn't have been possible before.

Something you can do in less than 5 minutes

Offer public appreciation for someone's work on Twitter or LinkedIn.

Public feedback is a way to share that someone has done something worth your gratitude. You don't do it to get a reply. You do it because it's a nice thing to do, and if someone does reply, that's a bonus.

For example, I tweeted that I was enjoying reading *The Happiness Project*, an excellent book by Gretchen Rubin. Although I was glad she responded, it was enough for me to know I was sharing something useful with my network.

7

Visible Work

Sharks in Western Australia are now tweeting out where they are.

ALAN YU, NPR

DURING A PERIOD when six of twenty fatal shark attacks around the world were in Australia, researchers there sought to find better ways of making the presence of sharks more visible to swimmers in the area.

So they put the sharks on Twitter.

Not that long ago, the only way swimmers would know if a shark was around was if a person nearby spotted one and yelled "Shark!" But waiting until someone within earshot sees a big dorsal fin is both scary and ineffective. You need a better way to know when a shark is nearby, and a better way to spread the word.

That led the researchers to tag hundreds of sharks with transmitters. Now, whenever one of the tagged sharks comes within half a mile of the beach, the transmitter triggers an alert to the forty-five thousand followers of the Surf Life Saving Western Australia Twitter feed, noting the shark's breed and approximate location. This and other beach safety and shark conservation groups (such as Shark Spotters in South Africa) also rely on humans at specific monitoring lookouts to find sharks and use Twitter to spread the word.

If sharks can do it . . .

The point of this story is to demonstrate how absurdly easy it is to be visible online. You can choose not to be visible, of course, and there are certainly people who have a good career and life without using social tools. Nor does the use of Twitter and other social media eliminate the need for human beings to talk to each other. (If you're swimming near me and see a shark, please yell "Shark!" before you tweet it.) But using these technologies can further amplify who you are and what you do, expanding the set of possibilities for your network and your career. Used effectively, our interactions on social tools complement the fundamentals of relationships that Dale Carnegie and Keith Ferrazzi have written about, significantly extending our reach.

The examples in this chapter are based on my experience using collaboration platforms inside a large global company, as well as the use of public social media. These examples illustrate how making yourself and your work visible can help you solve problems, innovate, and generally feel better about what you do every day.

Although these benefits may seem obvious, there are two objections I hear regularly.

Common objection #1: "I don't like social media."

I understand that some of you, with good reason, may have an almost allergic reaction to social technologies, especially public social media platforms like Facebook or Twitter. Maybe you think they're a waste of time, or that they can be toxic. Maybe you're right.

If you feel this way, you should know that *you don't need to use social tools to Work Out Loud.* You can make your work visible in person or via email. (The story of Mari, at the end of this chapter, is a good example of this.) There have been adaptations of WOL Circles in manufacturing plants and hospitals, where employees don't even have corporate email accounts or access to computers at work. The reason I include so many examples using social tools is that, unlike interactions in person or via email, they allow you to reach more people, including people you don't know. In addition, whatever you share can be discovered by others in the future. If you're adamant that social tools aren't for you, that's okay. You can start by using whatever you're comfortable with.

Common objection #2: "I'm an introvert."

Over twenty-four million people have watched Susan Cain's TED talk, "The Power of Introverts."[1]

In a culture where being social and outgoing are prized above all else, it can be difficult, even shameful, to be an introvert. But... introverts bring extraordinary talents and abilities to the world, and should be encouraged and celebrated.

In her book *Quiet*, she makes a convincing argument that the "rise of the Extrovert Ideal" undervalues a whole class of people who think and work in a more subdued way:[2]

At least one-third of the people we know are introverts. They are the ones who prefer listening to speaking, reading to partying; who innovate and create but dislike self-promotion; who favor working on their own over brainstorming in teams. Although they are often labeled "quiet," it is to introverts that we owe many of the great contributions to society—from van Gogh's sunflowers to the invention of the personal computer.

For sure, we can't afford to exclude or undervalue people. Yet if you consider yourself an introvert, I suggest WOL can be *especially* useful for you. Why? Because for much of the twentieth century, getting attention at work meant you had to speak up. Whether it was in a meeting of a few people or a few hundred, you had to find ways to make your views known. To do that, you had to sound smart in public and be more social or more aggressive. You had to be the "Extrovert Ideal" described in Cain's book.

But WOL emphasizes generosity, not self-promotion. The element of Visible Work isn't about you. It's about framing what you're doing as a contribution, something that might be helpful to others.

When I was advocating the use of an enterprise social network (a collaboration platform with social features such as sharing and commenting) in my company, I asked those who self-identified as introverts what they thought. They talked about the advantages of using social tools.

- *"It's easier to participate in online platforms than in live situations."*
- *"I'm more confident online than I am in real life."*
- *"It doesn't take the same type of emotional energy to connect with people online."*

One colleague, who describes herself as a "confirmed introvert," went even further:

It's a huge help. Without a tool like this, no one would know who I am or what I work on. I'd be hidden at my desk because I'm not outgoing enough to get out there and do things the typical extrovert way. It gives me a safe and controlled environment to present myself and my work.

Susan Cain is right. We need the introverts. We need to value people more for their ideas than for how smart they sound in public, more for their contributions than for their social skills—and WOL can help.

Social tools are increasingly being used for work

Social tools include online communities, blogs, Twitter, Facebook, collaboration platforms inside firms, and a growing list of technologies that are helping people to be visible and make connections. Each tool has its own features and benefits. The collaboration platform that Nikolay, Mara, and I used, for example, has some very real functional advantages over traditional intranet and email, since it provides searchable access to deep, structured expertise and also to flows of easy-to-skim information that make it simple to discover people and knowledge.

Andrew McAfee, author of *Enterprise 2.0*, wrote about the use of social tools inside companies and how they "simultaneously advance your own work, make your existence and expertise better known throughout a digital community, and benefit the organization as a whole."[3] Around the time that book came out, more people started writing about "narrating your work"[4] and "observable work."[5] Bryce Williams wrote his blog post about "working out loud."[6] And I attempted to introduce an enterprise social network where I was working.

Significantly improving how people get things done

Our early efforts failed to attract much interest. Although some colleagues were enthusiastic about the new social tools I introduced at the bank, most didn't see the point of adding yet another thing to do to their already busy day. Or, worse, they would dismiss it as "Facebook for work" without knowing much about it. Even those who were comfortable using social media relegated the tools to purely personal use and didn't think of applying them to their everyday work.

Over several years, though, we gradually learned how to realize the potential of these platforms in ways that were more convenient and comfortable for more people. To make our case to skeptical employees, one of the first things we learned was to stop using the word "social" and talk instead about the work that individuals and teams did every day. We would start with some facts about the most common tools they were using already: email and meetings. Here are some statistics we would share:[7]

- Professionals, managers, and salespeople spend 28 percent of their time reading or writing email.
- They spend another 19 percent of their time trying to track down information.
- People check their email thirty-six times per hour.

Most people could recognize themselves in these statistics, and they could see how changing those numbers would be good for them, as well as for the company. Not only was their individual time filled with interruptions and low-value activities, the knowledge of the firm also wasn't being captured anywhere except in people's inboxes. That knowledge couldn't be searched or built on by others in the company, and it effectively evaporated when the person left. It's not an exaggeration to say "email is where knowledge goes to die."[8]

Then we would talk about alternatives. Even if the majority of people at work aren't comfortable blogging or tweeting, everybody works. They create documents and presentations, organize meetings, attend events, and work on projects. They learn from books, classes, and colleagues. We would demonstrate how social tools could make all of that visible and more useful. It isn't about giving you yet more tasks or lumping social stuff onto your already crowded to-do list. It's about increasing both the supply and demand of knowledge so that everyone can be more effective.

Real benefits of making work visible in a big company

In *Reinventing Organizations*, Frederic Laloux shares case studies of companies who "achieved extraordinary breakthroughs in collaboration." Buurtzorg, a pioneering health-care organization based in the Netherlands, was one of those companies. Instead of the usual organizational hierarchy, Buurtzorg comprises thousands of self-managing teams, and each team "decides how they organize the work, share responsibilities and make decisions."[9] The results are extraordinary:[10]

- Client satisfaction rates are the highest of any health-care organization.

- Staff engagement is high. Buurtzorg has been voted Best Employer four out of the last five years.

- They're more efficient, having reduced costs for the Dutch health care system by 40 percent.

Here's an excerpt from a KPMG case study:[11]

Essentially, the program empowers nurses (rather than nursing assistants or cleaners) to deliver all the care that patient's need. And while this has meant higher costs per hour, the results have been fewer hours in total. Indeed, by changing the model of care, Buurtzorg has accomplished a 50 percent reduction in hours of care, improved quality of care and raised work satisfaction for employees.

Almost all of the case studies in *Reinventing Organizations* relied on some kind of collaboration platform or social intranet, and they all had a culture where employees were motivated to contribute.[12]

From Buurtzorg's inception, Jos de Blok envisioned that the "BuurtzorgWeb" would be a critical piece in the company's self-managing puzzle. The alternative— attempting to centralize knowledge within a staff of experts—would most likely be less effective and more costly. Above all, it would undermine the sense of pride Buurtzorg's nurses feel that they are the experts and collectively have invaluable knowledge to offer one another.

Collectively, the thousands of health-care professionals at Buurtzorg have an extraordinary breadth of medical and technical knowledge. Their internal social network helps employees locate a colleague with a specific expertise. It allows them to post questions directly in a continuous Facebook-like stream and get answers within hours or less. It allows them to organize knowledge online so others can find answers more quickly the next time and continuously improve them.

When we first introduced a social collaboration platform[13] where I worked, it was still something of a novelty. But now almost every company has some kind of interactive intranet, one that allows you to write and store documents, create groups and websites, start discussions, create events, and more. Most also allow you to comment and "like" almost anything, and to see all of your updates in a stream of activity similar to Facebook or Twitter.

In just over two years, fifty thousand people at our company were regularly using the social platform, and the number eventually approached one hundred thousand. Some employees used it just to search for information. Others used it as a more convenient way to share work with their team. Each month we would interview someone who was actively making their work visible and ask why they did it and how work changed for them. The benefits fell into four main categories:

- Becoming more visible
- Getting useful feedback

- Becoming more efficient
- Enjoying work more

Becoming more visible

Jennifer summed up the feelings of most people when she said, "The platform made it easier to connect with people who I might not have connected to otherwise and to get information and inputs from new places." Will, who worked in another area of the firm, said, "Using the platform introduced me to a lot of individuals across product lines and helped me understand more about different areas of the business. You get to see a lot of talent across the division you might not have seen otherwise."

People found that making their work visible helped them shape their reputation with a wider audience. Andreas in Germany noted, "Within my regular contacts, I was regarded for my expertise. However, I wasn't recognized by my indirect managers or anyone else with whom I had no direct contact." He was asked by his manager to "show more presence," and by using the platform to respond to questions and help people, he was able to do exactly that. "I was engaged in global discussions and able to help people with my expertise."

Getting useful feedback

An executive who was already an effective communicator found she could extend her reach and get valuable feedback compared to using more traditional channels, including email. "Once we were on the social platform, we started reaching a wider audience and getting tremendous feedback. It's extraordinary the people I've come across as a result of Working Out Loud." For some, the feedback they received helped improve their work. A manager whose team made their work visible on the collaboration platform said, "We went from the attitude 'be careful how you use it' to using it under certain circumstances to insisting that everyone use it to engage with our stakeholders." The reason is that it made their work better:

The number of different perspectives you can get on the problems you're trying to solve is always going to lead you to a better decision ... It has improved the quality of our work because of the feedback sought and provided via the platform. In addition, Working Out Loud really helps drive a collaborative and merit-based performance culture—it makes it far easier for the team to see what everyone is working on and to contribute to others' objectives.

That last part—making it easier to see what others are working on—is what makes it possible to increase collaboration and innovation across an organization. WOL helps increase both the supply and demand of knowledge in a company. When more work is visible, and more of the employees are used to searching for what's already been tried before, people are less likely to duplicate the same efforts and same mistakes, and more likely to build connections that can advance the work.

Becoming more efficient

Our team expected those first two benefits and were happy to see people realizing them. But we wanted more. We wanted to help people make their work more efficient. So we were gratified to hear from Michelle that "once you're connected with people and groups that are of value to you, you can see what's happening, which can help you in your role." For her, it wasn't about simply *more* connections, but rather about connections with relevant people who could help her get better at her job. Alun described how he used to email spreadsheets around and juggle multiple updates from multiple people. Now, by sharing his work online, everyone could see what had been updated and what hadn't. "An arduous process had been made more efficient, and it also has the benefit of being visible to everyone involved. My manager can go to one place and see the whole status and when it was last updated. He doesn't need to call me to chase down an answer. It's all right there." In Nikolay's community, as well as other role-based communities, we routinely saw experts coming together to solve problems and make improvements to processes. Because it was all visible, others could easily find it and build on it.

Some of you may feel that these capabilities aren't terribly new, and you'd be right. But as William Gibson famously said, "The future is already here—it's just not evenly distributed." That's especially true in most workplaces.

Enjoying work more

The fourth category of benefits surprised me. Some people—not everyone, but certainly a critical mass of people—started to like work more. I liked work more too, but I thought it might be because I had stumbled onto some particularly gratifying work. Others found different reasons, including that the collaboration platform made work easier, and it felt good to connect with people around the firm. My favorite reaction was from Derek, who posted this about the platform after having an epiphany of sorts about the power of making his work visible:

The best thing I have seen from the firm in my twenty-six years here.

I knew about the platform and maybe visited it a few times but certainly never posted. I didn't think I needed to. Just how wrong can one person be? After a fairly blunt conversation with my manager, I realized I needed to "sell" myself more . . . In the twenty-six years I have been employed here, I have worked in a number of roles in a few different countries and never thought anyone who needed my skills didn't know who I was. Once again, I was wrong.

So, blunt conversation fresh in my mind, let's "sell" myself. I thought about how I could do this and of course came across the social platform.

I soon came to realize that it isn't about selling yourself, it's about everything.

In the three or four weeks I've been using it regularly...

- *I've helped some people out.*
- *I've contributed to conversations from people I don't (or didn't) know.*
- *I've made friends (I've got twenty-six followers currently).*
- *I've got some new LinkedIn connections.*
- *I've publicized some vendor information relevant to my job.*
- *I am following thirty-five people, and I feel like I know people now.*

Did I sell myself? I think I did but in a nice way. I certainly feel like I am contributing to the firm more, and other people know who I am and what I can offer the firm.

Paul has more impact, recognition, and fun at work

Paul is someone who experienced all of these benefits. When he started using the social collaboration platform, he was in his mid-forties, working in a communications group. Paul is the kind of person who doesn't talk about himself and isn't an active user of social media. He began just by posting material related to his projects, such as ways to make the firm's intranet less expensive. His intended audience was an online community of communications people analogous to Jordi Muñoz's online drone community. At first, a few people provided support, suggestions, and referrals to others who might be interested. But each time someone commented or liked his proposals, more people became aware of Paul and his work.

Whenever someone helped him, Paul would use the collaboration platform to publicly recognize the person and their contribution, further spreading the word and motivating people to help him even more. Within a few months, he had built a small online movement that saved his firm over $500,000. "I probably got this done ten times quicker than I might have through traditional channels," he said. More and more people, including a managing director from another division, became aware of Paul through his work online. "I know you," people would say when they met him. "Your name keeps coming up."

Looking back, it's actually been a great way to get "known." I now have people proactively reaching out to me because they've heard my name attached to the project. On our collaboration platform, you can create a personal brand for yourself.

Paul's personal brand wasn't based on spin or clever marketing of himself, but on his work and the value other people saw in it. His ability to build a network and solicit feedback and ideas made him more effective at his job. Based on all of this, Paul was asked to take on additional responsibilities that went well beyond his original role.

His team even won an industry award for their innovative approach, expanding his reputation outside the company.

Mari makes her world bigger

Most of the examples in this chapter are based on using a collaboration platform inside an organization. But what if your company doesn't have one, or you don't work inside a big company? Or what if you're just not ready to be visible? The story of someone in my own WOL Circle illustrates how even small steps can increase your odds and make other steps possible.

Mari is a piano teacher in New York City, and she's extremely good with children. She's also an extraordinarily talented musician. Despite her small frame, she plays with a forceful passion and strength. Yet one night, as a group of us were talking about work, she shared something that surprised us.

My world is too small.

How could that be? Mari's students adore her, and she seems to enjoy her work so much. But, that night, she told us she yearned for interactions with people beyond the same families she met each week. What she most enjoyed doing, she said, was composing, and she wanted to do more of it. As much as she liked teaching, she wanted to have people hear her own music.

Mari wasn't comfortable with being visible or talking about her work. She was shy and felt her English wasn't good enough. (Her native language is Japanese.) The prospect of writing a blog post or starting a YouTube channel was too foreign to her, and she felt she "wasn't that kind of person."

In our Circle, she started with small steps, writing down the names of people from music school she had lost touch with and reconnecting with some of them. She played internet detective, searching for people who might be interested in her music. That's how she discovered independent filmmakers who needed musical scores. It took her several weeks to work up the courage to reach out to a particular director via email, sharing a piece she created: "I've enjoyed your films, and I thought this music I composed might be useful." That led to an email exchange, and then to working together.

In the years after our Circle ended, Mari kept taking more steps. She began experimenting with iTunes, YouTube, Spotify, and other tools, and released an album online. One of her pieces, a trio for piano, was performed by a youth group in Boston. A solo piece won "The Contemporary Piano," an international competition. Yet another has been selected by RMN Classical to be included in a new compilation album.[14]

"You made my world bigger," Mari told me. But it wasn't me. She did it herself with help from a small, trusted Circle. That experience gave her the confidence to voice a goal and take steps toward it.

Focus on the contribution

One day I was working in the Poets House in my neighborhood (a national poetry library and literary center) and I noticed some poems on display written by children. One by Allan, a fourth-grader at PS1, was about the Statue of Liberty. Janice compared NYC to a grizzly bear, and Leah wrote about immigrants and called her poem "Welcome New Americans!" ("Welcome Immigrants! You are imported good!") I took photos and shared one of the poems on Instagram, along with a question:

Ever notice how most children proudly make their work visible and most adults don't?

A friend commented: "Because they don't have the fear of rejection yet."

That made me think of the resistance people might have to Visible Work, and how daunting it might feel. Just as it can't be about megaphones and self-promotion, it can't be about acceptance and rejection either. Instead of anticipating applause or any other response, your intention is simply to offer something of yourself as a gift:

I tried this.
I made this.
I learned this.
I enjoyed this.
I hope you like it or find it useful.

I like to think the phrase "Working Out Loud" can give you the same feeling you have when you listen to someone read out loud, perhaps a poem or short story, or when you read a book to your child. "Out Loud," in that context, can make the work come alive, and sharing it can be the basis of a connection, something that brings people closer.

How much you share, how you share it, and with whom you share it are all up to you. The point is that it's easier and more commonplace than ever to make you and your work visible, and doing so provides you with substantial benefits. The next and final element, A Growth Mindset, will help you continue practicing until it becomes a habit.

KEY IDEAS IN THIS CHAPTER

- The shark story demonstrates how easy it is to be visible online.

- Contributions are like pebbles in a pond, rippling out and bringing you into contact with more people and possibilities.

- Visible Work helps you make more connections, improve the quality of your work, become more efficient, and enjoy work more.

- When people make their work visible, some show finished products and many narrate their work in progress. *This is how I did that. This is what I did and why. This is what I learned that might help you too.*

- Social tools are a means, not an end. You don't have to use them, but your online contributions amplify who you are and what you do, they extend your reach, and they expand the set of contributions you can make and how you can offer them.

- WOL isn't about megaphones and self-promotion. It's about offering something of yourself as a gift, about being helpful without the expectation of applause.

EXERCISES

Something you can do in less than a minute

Imagine someone meets you at a meeting or event and then searches for you on the internet to find your contact information or to learn more about you. What would you want them to find?

Wherever you happen to be now, use your phone or favorite internet device to search for yourself. Are the results you're looking at what you would like others to see? How much of your best work is visible?

Something you can do in less than 5 minutes

A few years ago, I searched for myself on the internet and was disappointed to find an old article about some work I did, and some stepper exercise equipment. Search for me now, and you'll see work I'm proud of.

Search for people you find particularly interesting—people whose work you admire, as opposed to celebrities. What's their online presence like? Is it easy to find them and their work?

8

A Growth Mindset

I've missed more than 9,000 shots in my career.
I've lost almost 300 games. Twenty-six times,
I've been trusted to take the game-winning shot and
missed. I've failed over and over and over again
in my life. And that is why I succeed.

MICHAEL JORDAN, FOR NIKE

DEVELOPING A GROWTH mindset is one of the few things commonly taught to students as well as to employees of all ages. I've seen posters for it in my son's elementary school and also in the halls of large corporations like Daimler. It is a mindset of improvement, and it's one of the most important elements for making your WOL practice sustainable. There are three reasons for this:

1   A focus on *getting better* versus *being good* reduces the fear normally associated with trying to improve

your work or relationships, enabling you to experiment and learn more.

2 Over time your improved capabilities give you a sense of confidence that makes further improvement more likely. That enables you to make more valuable contributions.

3 As you seek to improve yourself, you share your learning with others so they can also benefit. That reinforces the element of generosity.

To begin to understand how to develop an effective, sustainable approach to growing and improving, it turns out we can all learn a lot from a group of ten-year-olds.

Focusing on learning
makes a fundamental difference

Researchers Carol Dweck and Claudia Mueller from Columbia University worked with fifth-graders in a small midwestern US town and several cities in the northeast to understand the effects of different kinds of praise on motivation. In one study in the late 1990s,[1] they gave children three sets of problems: an easy set, a very difficult set, and another easy set. After the first set, all students were individually told they solved at least 80 percent of the problems they answered, no matter what their actual score was. Some students were praised for their ability ("You must be really smart!"), and some were praised for their effort ("You must have worked really hard!"). Then the researchers asked each child a range of questions, such as how much they enjoyed working on the problems and the kind of problems they would prefer to see in the next set.

The second set of problems was difficult, and the children were all told they performed "a lot worse," solving no more than half of them. The researchers again asked the children about the kinds of problems they would prefer and whether they would want to work on more of them. They also asked them why they thought they didn't do as well on the second set. Was it that they didn't work hard enough, weren't good enough at those problems, or didn't have enough time? Finally, the children worked on a third set of problems that was as easy as the original set.

The researchers aimed to measure whether the different kinds of praise after the first set of problems would affect how the children dealt with the setback in the second set. Would they perform differently on the third set? Would they choose easier problems? Would they view themselves differently?

The results, replicated in numerous studies, showed dramatic differences in performance. Children praised for being smart did 25 percent *worse* on the third set of problems compared to the first. Children praised for working hard performed 25 percent *better*. That's an incredible difference in performance. Even more fascinating were the other differences they found. The children praised for intelligence equated their performance with their ability. So they did all they could to maximize their performance relative to other children. They chose easier problems, asked about the performance of others, and even "misrepresented" their scores more than the other children. They had a fixed mindset, tending to describe intelligence as a trait you're born with and can't change much.

Children praised for their effort, however, equated their performance with how hard they worked. So they did all they could to maximize their learning. They chose problems that were more challenging. They were more interested in strategies for solving problems than in the scores of other students. They had a growth mindset, believing intelligence was something they could improve.

As you practice WOL, you want to be like the children praised for their effort. You want to have a growth mindset. You're not innately good or bad at building a network, at making your work visible, or at leading with generosity. You're just at a particular point in the process of learning, the process of getting better. No matter what skill you're trying to develop, you'll make more progress with less anxiety if you frame your improvement as a learning goal, worrying less about how good you are right now and focusing instead on getting better over time.

A method for getting better at anything

Albert Bandura, one of the world's most cited psychologists, developed a method he called "guided mastery" that's incredibly effective for developing new capabilities.

It's also the basis for Part III of this book, where you'll learn to Work Out Loud toward an individual goal.

In the 1960s, Bandura used this method to cure people of snake phobias in less than a few hours. Subjects would receive treatment combining "graduated live modeling with guided participation."[2] First, they would watch for fifteen minutes through a one-way mirror as the experimenter interacted with a snake. After the snake was back in its glass cage, the subject might enter the room and sit on a chair at varying distances from the cage. Gradually, the experimenter would model more and more interactions and help the subject follow along. It was the subjects who, based on their apprehensiveness, set the pace at which they proceeded. As they made progress overcoming their phobia, they noticed other changes too.

Having successfully eliminated a phobia that had plagued them for most of their lives, a number of subjects reported increased confidence that they could cope effectively with other fear-provoking events. As one subject explained it, "My success in gradually overcoming this fear of snakes has contributed to a greater feeling of confidence generally in my abilities to overcome any other problem that may arise. I have more faith in myself."

That feeling, in short, is one of high self-efficacy, a strong belief that you can accomplish a task or goal. People with such a belief, like the fifth-graders in the study mentioned earlier, experience a wide range of benefits.[3]

A strong sense of efficacy enhances human accomplishment and personal well-being in many ways. People with high assurance in their capabilities approach difficult tasks as challenges to be mastered rather than as threats to be avoided. Such an efficacious outlook fosters intrinsic interest and deep engrossment in activities. They set themselves challenging goals and maintain strong commitment to them. They heighten and sustain their efforts in the face of failure. They quickly recover their sense of efficacy after failures or setbacks. They attribute failure to insufficient effort or deficient knowledge and skills that are acquirable. They approach threatening situations with assurance that they can exercise control over them. Such an efficacious outlook produces personal accomplishments, reduces stress, and lowers vulnerability to depression.

People who Work Out Loud report this same feeling of self-efficacy. In developing the habit of regularly contributing to their network, they become more effective, more connected, and more confident. Joyce, for example, was able to model what others were doing with social media, try things herself, and gradually develop a sense that she too could do it. Jordi Muñoz got the benefits of guided mastery by seeing what others did, submitting his own drone designs, and getting feedback on how to improve them. Now, more than four decades after Bandura's work, millions of people are using a new kind of guided mastery to increase their self-efficacy while they get better at everything from art history to Python programming.

A modern form of guided mastery that helps kids learn

Back in 2004, a hedge fund analyst in Boston with three degrees from MIT and a Harvard MBA started tutoring his young cousins in New Orleans. His name is Salman Khan. To supplement the lessons, he posted some videos on YouTube, and his cousins told him they preferred the videos over talking to him live because they could watch them at their own pace and at convenient times. To his surprise, other students stumbled onto the videos and posted comments about how helpful they were, so Khan kept recording lessons on a wider range of topics.

Over time, the audience grew and provided more feedback on what was working and not working. Salman Khan's goal shifted from helping his cousins to helping kids around the world, and Khan Academy was born. He persisted, posting hundreds and ultimately thousands of lessons. As the library grew, so did the audience and so did the number of opportunities. His work started to attract the attention of teachers and others interested in improving education. To complement the videos, Khan Academy eventually produced software that helped students track how well they were doing and where they needed help. Then they created dashboards for teachers that use Khan Academy in the classroom. Kids would watch lectures before class, freeing teachers to focus their in-class time on customized coaching for each child, based on the data in the dashboard. More feedback led to more ideas and improvements, such as the ability for other students to become coaches and earn points and badges in the process. The teachers got feedback on their work too, so they could also improve.

Below is an excerpt from the Khan Academy vision statement.[4] Notice how the phrases echo Bandura's description of guided mastery for both the student and the teacher.

Our vision for Khan Academy in the classroom includes:

- *Individualizing learning by replacing one-size-fits-all lectures with self-paced learning*

- *Taking a mastery-based approach to learning critical knowledge and skills (every student takes as long as he/she needs to learn each concept fully)*

- *Creating collaborative learning environments with students solving problems together and tutoring one another*

- *Using focused coaching by the teacher to address students' individual needs*

- *Providing guidance to the teacher through real-time metrics and reporting on student performance*

Sitting in his hedge fund office, it might have seemed impossible for Salman Khan to create a global online education movement. But by now the pattern is familiar. He had a modest goal. He made his work visible and framed it as a contribution. Those contributions led to new connections and feedback that made his work better, and that in turn led to him making more contributions and connecting with more people. Combined, his increased effectiveness and a bigger, better network led to more possibilities.

On YouTube alone, Khan Academy now has almost five million subscribers and five hundred million views of its library. When Salman Khan told his story in a TED talk, Bill Gates joined him on stage at the end, applauding his work and telling the audience, "It's amazing. I think you just got a glimpse at the future of education."

Creating a growth mindset

Just as Albert Bandura saw improvement in a wide range of people, so did Salman Khan, further reinforcing that guided mastery could help anyone get better. Khan saw in students what Carol Dweck and Claudia Mueller saw in their fifth-grade research subjects—that focusing on improvement instead of performance can make a huge difference in effectiveness and confidence over time.[5]

There's a group of kids who've raced ahead, and there's a group of kids who are a little bit slower. And in a traditional model, if you did a snapshot assessment, you said, "these are the gifted kids," "these are the slow kids" ... But when you let every student work at their own pace— and we see it over and over and over again—you see students who took a little bit of extra time on one concept or the other, but once they get through that concept, they race ahead. And so the same kids you thought were slow, you now would think they're gifted.

You can experience this same pattern as you Work Out Loud. Put in terms of guided mastery, you can readily come into contact with experts modeling the work at which you're trying to get better. You'll make your work visible in small steps and get feedback on that work, making progress at your own pace. All the while, you'll be strengthening your self-efficacy. But all of this hinges on you believing that you can develop new skills and habits, that you have a mindset of getting better. Following a process of guided mastery for one goal—whether you're overcoming a phobia or the challenges of trigonometry—will give you confidence to attempt other goals.

How do you develop such a mindset? Heidi Grant Halvorson, who was a graduate student at Columbia when the experiments were done with the fifth-graders, went on to conduct her own experiments and write an extremely useful book called *Succeed: How We Can Reach Our Goals*. In one of the books she contributed to, she lists five ways to shift your mindset:[6]

1 Give yourself permission to make mistakes.
2 Ask for help when you run into trouble.
3 Focus on your own progress instead of comparing yourself to others.

4 Think in terms of progress, not perfection.
5 Examine your beliefs and, when necessary, challenge them.

That last one is perhaps the most fundamental. Study after study has shown how labels applied to you (by you or by others) can become self-fulfilling prophecies that unnecessarily limit what you can achieve. You need to be on the lookout for such self-limiting beliefs and get in the habit of challenging them:

Whether it's intelligence, creativity, self-control, charm, or athleticism—the science shows our abilities to be profoundly malleable. When it comes to mastering any skill, your experience, effort, and persistence matter a lot... So the next time you find yourself thinking, "But I'm just not good at this," remember: you're just not good at it yet.

Putting the five elements into practice

Thirty-one years after the snake phobia study, Bandura wrote "Cultivate Self-Efficacy for Personal and Organizational Effectiveness," in which he shows how guided mastery in the workplace enhanced not only self-efficacy but also emotional well-being, satisfaction, and level of productivity.[8] When you work in a way that's more open, generous, and connected, your work can be much more than a job. It can be an integral part of a richer life.

Part III of this book is about experiencing your own guided mastery program, learning to put the five elements of WOL into practice so you too can realize the benefits Bandura described, and earn Fortune's expensive smile.

KEY IDEAS IN THIS CHAPTER

- Focus on getting better instead of being good. Research shows how emphasizing improvement instead of performance can make a significant difference in effectiveness and confidence.

- Guided mastery—gradual, self-paced practice in which you model others and get feedback along the way—is an extremely effective method for developing new capabilities.

- Whether you're overcoming a phobia or the challenges of trigonometry, following a process of guided mastery for one particular goal will give you confidence to attempt other goals.

- The next time you find yourself thinking, "I'm just not good at this," remember: you're just not good at it *yet*.

EXERCISES

Something you can do in less than a minute
Think of three things you read recently that helped you learn something. Now use Twitter to search for the people who wrote those things and follow them.

Something you can do in less than 5 minutes
Subscribe to at least one blog. You can receive weekly posts related to WOL by submitting your email address at working outloud.com/blog. Or search for other blogs that inspire you or are related to your goals and interests.

I enjoy Seth Godin's daily posts at seths.blog in particular. Here's a quote from one called "The Tragedy of Small Expectations": [9]

If we can help just one person refuse to accept false limits, we've made a contribution. If we can give people the education, the tools and the access they need to reach their goals, we've made a difference.

PART III

Your Own Guided Mastery Program

9

New Skills, Habits, and Mindset in 12 Weeks

A journey of a thousand miles begins with a single step.

LAO TZU

DO YOU REMEMBER the movie *300*? It depicted the Battle of Thermopylae in 480 BC where, in a mountain pass, three hundred Spartans stood their ground against more than a hundred thousand Persians for three full days. In addition to the extraordinary story, the movie was famous for the physical conditioning of the male actors. The lead actor, Gerard Butler, and all the other men in the film had lean, chiseled bodies that appealed to a wide audience and helped the film gross over $450,000,000 worldwide.

At the time, all the men I knew, including me, were envious. We wanted bodies like that. We were amazed to learn that all the actors achieved their physiques in just eight to twelve weeks. Even better, all the information about the workouts they did was online. Any of us could follow the instructions and have the body we said we wanted.

None of us did.

Why not? It was too much, too soon. The workouts were described as "brutal." There were even health warnings. As much as we thought we'd like to sport physiques like those we saw in the movie, we never moved a muscle.

Touching the treadmill

Martha Beck, "America's most famous life coach," routinely works with people who have personal development goals but are unable to make meaningful progress. Even a simple, practical goal like "I want to get in shape" can be problematic. We may have negative associations with the effort required to get in shape. *"I hate exercise."* We may not believe we're capable. *"I'm not an exercise person."* We may not have the knowledge or the environment we need. *"I just don't have the time."*

Any of these is enough to stop you from making much progress. Combined, you won't get off the couch. What Martha Beck taught me was to break down the goal and begin with a small step so simple it verges on ridiculous.

Can't go for a run four times a week for an hour? Try once a week. Still too much? Go for fifteen minutes. Not working for you? Walk to the treadmill and touch it every day.

Touching the treadmill won't improve your cardio-vascular function, but it will make it possible to bypass your hardwired aversion to change. Early in human history, major changes were a threat. When we would see a saber-toothed tiger, the blood would flow to the base of our brain, which regulates our fight-or-flight mechanisms. The thinking parts would practically shut off.

Today, our bodies react that same way when faced with big, audacious goals. Seth Godin refers to it as "the lizard brain." Steven Pressfield calls it "the resistance." It's a common and natural reaction to change. The more evolved part of our brains really does want us to achieve our goals—to develop new capabilities that can make life richer (and longer)—but the part of our brains we carry with us from long ago is trying to protect us. When we reframe our goals in ways that make them less scary, ways that don't activate our fight-or-flight mechanism, we increase our chances of making progress.

A guided mastery program for WOL

Before I started writing this book, I tried a variety of techniques to help people change how they work: creating helpful guides, conducting individual one-hour sessions, organizing meet-ups, even teaching a three-month course. None of this produced as much change as I had hoped. Though most people understood the concepts and liked the *idea* of Working Out Loud, it was just too hard for them to change their habits.

Looking back, my teaching was often the verbal equivalent of handing out live snakes in a roomful of people with snake phobias. Not very helpful. Telling colleagues they had to develop new ways of working put them on the defensive, even if they agreed. People need more than verbal persuasion to change behaviors; they need practical assistance. That's what led me to develop the steps you'll read about in the rest of Part III, and that are the basis of the WOL Circle method.

Your own 12-week program

Part III is intended to help you put the five elements of WOL into practice. Just as Albert Bandura used guided mastery to cure people of their phobias and increase people's sense of self-efficacy, you'll use guided mastery to develop the habit of Working Out Loud and experience a wide range of benefits for yourself.[1]

To get better results than I got after watching *300*, remember to have a growth mindset. Think of the exercises in the following chapters as small steps, a way for you to learn and explore. Whenever you hear your lizard brain talking about all the reasons you won't succeed, lull it back to sleep by telling it you're just experimenting.

Remind yourself that there's nothing to fear, really. Over twelve weeks, you'll try some new things, discover interesting people and ideas, and gradually develop a set of habits that are quite pleasant. By the time you realize that WOL may change your life, the lizard won't be able to stop you.

KEY IDEAS IN THIS CHAPTER

- You have a hardwired aversion to change, even to changes that may be positive for you in the long run.

- To avoid triggering your lizard brain, try "touching the treadmill," starting with a small, simple step toward your goal that allows you to get started.

- To further help you avoid the resistance to change, frame the entire process as a learning goal. Focus on getting better rather than being good.

EXERCISES

Something you can do in less than a minute
Look back at positive habits you have tried to develop—anything from flossing to playing the piano to exercising

regularly. Think about the times you achieved your goal and the times you didn't. What was the difference?

Something you can do in less than 5 minutes
Peer support helps you through the ups and downs of trying to change. Think of people you know who can provide positive, nonjudgmental support as you go through your own guided mastery program. They will be the kinds of people, for example, with whom you would be comfortable sharing ideas in this book. Write down their names.

☑ **GETTING STARTED**

☐ CONNECTING

☐ CREATING

☐ LEADING

10

A Practical Goal & Your First Relationship List

Deciding what we pay attention to can shape our entire worldview. It can determine which doors are open to us and which doors we never see.

WOL CIRCLE GUIDE

MUCH OF WHAT you'll be doing throughout Part III is based on asking yourself three questions:

1 What am I trying to accomplish?
2 Who can help me with my goal?
3 How can I contribute to them to deepen our relationship?

Choosing a goal, such as exploring a new area of interest or developing a skill at work, helps you decide which relationships you'll want to build and what contributions you'll make. It makes you purposeful instead of just busy. The goal you choose here isn't Your One Special Purpose In Life but something much simpler. Consider the goals of some of the people in the book so far:

- Sabine wanted to explore new HR methods.
- Anja wanted to explore using new technology.
- Mara wanted to learn more about building communities.
- Jordi wanted to learn more about drones.
- Joyce wanted to learn more about social media.
- Brandon wanted to explore becoming a photographer.
- Paul wanted to be more effective.
- I wanted to learn more about collaboration.

Do you see a pattern? The goals are largely about learning and exploring, and they have a certain Goldilocks nature about them: not too big, not too small. In the exercise to come, you'll choose your own goal. Here are a few questions that can guide you.

Do you care about it?

When you consider a goal, pay attention to how you feel. Is it something you're genuinely interested in, or rather something you feel you're supposed to want? Choosing a goal that you truly care about taps into your innate need for control, and that fuels your motivation to do the exercises and make progress. If your goal doesn't genuinely spark your interest, pick something else.

Can you benefit from the experience of others?

Deepening relationships is at the heart of WOL. You want to select a goal that depends on relationships giving you access to knowledge and opportunities you might not otherwise have. If your goal sounds like something you would accomplish on your own—"I will get a graduate degree," "I will get promoted"—try to express it in a way that captures how relationships can help you. For example, "I want to learn from others who have already accomplished what I would like to do."

Can you frame it as a learning goal?

Goals framed in terms of learning or exploration make it easier for you to adopt a growth mindset, try new things, and become open to new people and possibilities. Because such goals feel more flexible and less risky than other kinds of goals, they're less likely to trigger anxiety or resistance. Consider goals that start with one of these phrases:

- *"I would like to be better at..."*
- *"I would like to learn more about..."*
- *"I would like to know more people who..."*

Framed this way, you'll more readily tap into your needs for mastery (a sense of getting better at something) and purpose (your connection to other people, to meaning, or both).

Can you make progress toward it in twelve weeks?

Choose something achievable, or that you can at least make progress toward. If your goal is too vague, you'll have trouble identifying a specific set of people who can help you achieve it. If your goal is too ambitious, merely thinking of it can trigger resistance and prevent you from taking a step. If that's the case for you, consider reframing your goal into more achievable chunks or sub-goals. Once WOL is a habit, you can choose more ambitious goals.

Here are some common goals people choose in their Circle:

- I want to learn more about something I care about.
- I would like to explore possibilities in a new area.
- I want to meet people with similar interests.
- I want to get better at what I do for a living.
- I would like to find a new role.
- I would like to get more recognition in my current job.

Don't feel any pressure to get this exactly right. Almost any goal will help orient your activity through Part III. In my first WOL Circle, one person was thinking about becoming a financial advisor and wanted to explore that. Another person was passionate about making people aware of dangerous toxins in products and suggesting alternatives. One started an online fashion consulting business she wanted to grow, and another cared about educational issues. As you Work Out Loud toward a particular goal, you'll be developing skills, habits, and a mindset that will help you with almost any goal in the future.

EXERCISE: Your goal for Part III (5 minutes)
Take time now to think about your goal for the next twelve weeks, and write it down. Keep it to just a sentence or two.

In the next twelve weeks, I want to:

_____

_____

_____

If that wasn't easy for you, or if you're uncertain about the goal you wrote down, that's okay. There is no right or wrong when it comes to the goal you pick now. You'll reflect on it and possibly adapt or change it in the coming chapters.

Three examples

Hayley's goal was clear. She had decided to move back to her native Australia, and was heading to a beautiful area near the Coral Sea appropriately named the Gold Coast. So, she described her goal this way:

I want to build a purposeful network of people on the Gold Coast that I would enjoy working with, and to find a role in a company that's aligned to my overall purpose and passions.

That's a good goal. It's straightforward, something she cares about, and she can make meaningful progress toward it in twelve weeks.

Vincent took a bit longer to choose his goal. He is an engineer who had worked in manufacturing before transitioning to a quality management department, so he was changing jobs as well as countries. At first, he was unsure whether his goal should be related to his skills, his new role, or his new location. But when he was told that one of his group's responsibilities was to "introduce social media for collaboration with the other departments," he decided to pick a goal related to that:

I want to set up a personal blog which enables me to share my work with others, and to contribute to communities that will enable me to connect with people I don't know yet.

Barbara struggled to choose a goal. She's one of the first people I ever coached, and when I talked to her she was working in Frankfurt in a group responsible for her company's books and records, spending a lot of time analyzing large, complicated spreadsheets. We discussed a wide range of possible goals. Did she want more money or recognition at work? A different job in finance? Not really. When she mentioned she enjoyed helping people with taxes, I asked if exploring that could be her goal, but that wasn't appealing either. Barbara said she actually didn't consider herself a finance person. Though she thought she was good at it, particularly the detailed analysis, it wasn't *her*. "I just sort of stumbled into it after university," she said, and she didn't know how or when to change. She said she wanted "to see what else is out there," but that seemed too vague.

Barbara was stuck. That's when I asked about her interests outside of work. Immediately, she started talking about a hobby of hers: genealogy. For Barbara, this was about much more than charting a family tree. She would spend hours poring over old church and government records, for example, and calling archivists for possible leads when she hit a dead end. In addition to researching her own family, she looked up historical figures and particular dates in history, and blogged regularly about what she found, just for fun. Finally, it was obvious what her goal should be.

I want to find other people who share my passion for genealogy and explore possibilities related to that.

You might wonder whether this is a suitable goal for Working Out Loud. After all, what does a genealogy hobby have to do with work? The reason it's a good goal is that, by choosing something she cares about, Barbara is much more likely to put the five elements into practice. Doing so will help her build the skills of finding people related to a topic and building relationships that increase the chance of information exchange, cooperation, and collaboration. She will develop habits and a mindset she can apply to any goal, and that's good for her as well as for her company.

Questions, questions, questions

Whenever I work with companies or present to an audience, they have the chance to ask questions and raise issues, and the ensuing exchange helps us explore a topic further. To give you a sense of what that's like, and perhaps anticipate what you might be thinking as you read and do the exercises, I'll include common questions and comments throughout Part III. Here are two questions related to writing down your goal:

Q: What if I don't know my goal?

For many people, it's far from obvious what to choose as a goal. Abraham Maslow, the psychologist famous for defining our hierarchy of needs, said, "It isn't normal to know what we want. It is a rare and difficult psychological achievement." If you don't have a specific goal in mind, consider one of the common goals listed on page 150. Or, like Barbara, choose a goal that piques your interest and curiosity. Don't worry about picking the best goal. Focus instead on choosing something that will make doing the exercises feel enjoyable and worthwhile.

Q: What if I pick the wrong one?

There is no right or wrong when it comes to goals. If you discover that you're not as interested in a given goal as you thought you would be, that's okay. You can change it. Part of Purposeful Discovery is refining your sense of what you like and don't like, and it's not uncommon for people in WOL Circles to adapt or change their goals over the course of the twelve weeks.

Finding people related to your goal

Remember the second question at the beginning of this chapter: "Who can help me with my goal?" The answer to that question is in a simple relationship list that you create. With your goal in mind, here are the kinds of people you'll put on your list:

- People who have done something similar to what you would like to do

- People you have learned from

- People inside your company whose interests or role relates to your goal

- People who have written or given talks about something related to your goal

Hayley, for example, used Google to find winners of the Gold Coast Business Excellence Awards, the Chamber of Commerce, the Gold Coast Business Directory, and other existing networks of companies based on the Gold Coast. That's how she found Billabong, SurfStitch, and other firms in the area. Then she went to their corporate sites to learn more about their work and about people employed there. She also found people by searching LinkedIn for these organizations. As she was searching, though, she found other promising results. The Gold Coast hosted the Commonwealth Games in 2018, something that appealed to Hayley's interest in health and exercise. Looking at the site for the games gave her some ideas, and led her to a two-minute YouTube interview with the head of marketing and communications for the games. He spoke about a range of work and challenges involved in preparing for such an event. Hayley thought it was interesting, relevant to her goal, and worth learning more about. So she put him on her list.

Vincent used his company's intranet to find people in quality management groups in other locations and divisions. He also searched LinkedIn for people working in quality management, and searched for blogs and online groups related to the topic. Barbara began by searching for other people like her, including other genealogy bloggers, people who organized genealogy conferences, and firms that specialized in family tree research.

EXERCISE: Your first relationship list (15 minutes)
Think of the list you create in this next exercise as a first draft. Over the course of your guided mastery program, your list will evolve as you explore and build relationships.

You'll probably think of some names for your list right away. Write them down. Then play internet detective and start searching for people related to your goal. What often happens is that, within a few minutes, you'll stumble across people and ideas you weren't aware of before. "Aha! They look interesting!"

Try to find at least ten people.

1 _____

2 _____

3 _____

4 _____

5 _____

6 _____

7 _____

8 _____

9 _____

10 _____

Q: What if I'm having trouble finding people?

Don't limit yourself to people you know. Practice your sleuthing skills: try different kinds of searches, use different tools, and scan the search results for clues that might lead to interesting connections. For example, once you find one interesting person, you might try to see who that person is connected to, and then keep following the trail.

Something important just happened

Have you ever noticed how, when you buy something new—a certain kind of car or stroller, a special dress or tie—you suddenly start noticing that same thing all around you? It's as if, because of a choice you made, the world suddenly conjures up more of that specific thing.[1]

It's not magic, it's neuroscience. Your choice primes your brain, and as a result you are literally more receptive to what you chose, so you see things you would have otherwise missed. The small steps you are taking in this chapter have attuned your attention, and in the weeks ahead you will be thinking more about your goal and about people related to it. You will become increasingly aware of their work, their thinking, and feedback from others about them. You will notice people and ideas you hadn't seen before. You will make connections you hadn't thought of, and start to think differently about your goal.

If you did both exercises—investing a grand total of about twenty minutes into a goal you care about—you've actually done more than most people do in a month. It's not that people are lazy or uncaring, it's just that the changes we want in our careers and our lives can seem so daunting that we don't even know where to begin.

By writing down a goal and listing people related to it, you've already "touched the treadmill" and made additional progress possible. Now you're ready to start answering the third question: "How can I contribute to them to deepen our relationship?"

KEY IDEAS IN THIS CHAPTER

- *What am I trying to accomplish?* Goals are typically about learning and exploring. You should pick something that you care about, that is reasonably specific, and that you can make progress toward in twelve weeks.

- *Who can help me with my goal?* Start by thinking of people who have done something similar, who you have learned from, whose interests or role relate to yours, or who have written or given talks about something related to your goal.

- By writing down a goal and listing people related to it, you have attuned your attention, enabling you to make connections to people and ideas related to your goal you may never have seen otherwise.

EXERCISES

Something you can do in less than a minute

Think about the goal you chose and hold it in your mind for a few seconds. How does it make you feel? If reflecting on your goal gives you a sense of burden or dread instead of curiosity and interest, consider choosing something else. Make that choice now.

Something you can do in less than 5 minutes

Review your relationship list. Try to add at least two more names. Each time you review your list you will further attune your attention, making it easier to make progress toward your goal.

11

Your First Contributions

If you always give, you will always have.

ANCIENT PROVERB

A GENEROUS PERSON can be defined as someone who shows a readiness to give more of something than is strictly necessary or expected. So when you are generous, what is the "something" you give more of? What is it that you have to offer?

Most people think far too narrowly about the answer to these questions. Sure, you can be generous with money or time, or with sharing information. But that is a tiny sliver of the spectrum of possible contributions you can make that others would value. The exercises to come will help you offer more of this spectrum and do so in a variety of ways. Over time, you'll realize that you have much more to offer than you might think—and that your contributions deepen a sense of trust and relatedness with more people.

In this chapter, you'll start with two universal gifts: attention and appreciation. But first, I ask that you try this exercise.

EXERCISE: The generosity test (3 minutes)

This is a simple test, and yet it's one I feel I need to keep taking. The more I practice, the more I see how it applies to things I do throughout the day and throughout my life. If you're like me, you might be disturbed by the results.

You can take the generosity test by imagining the scenario in your head or, even better, by actually doing it. Here is how it goes:

Hold the door open for someone you don't know. As you do it, pay close attention to what you're thinking the moment you decide to open the door, to the way you open it, and to the other person's reaction. Visualize it now. (You might want to close your eyes.)

If the other person thanks you, how did that make you feel? If they pass by without saying anything or even acknowledging you, does that change anything?

My results

Here's what I usually notice whenever I take this test.

1 I get a good feeling when I decide to open the door. *I'm about to do something nice.*

2   I make eye contact with the other person or say something to make sure they see me opening the door for them. *After you!*

3   When they thank me, I get another surge of good feeling. If they ignore me, however, I get irritated, even angry. *How rude!*

It has taken me a while to recognize I don't really open the door for the other person. I open it for myself, for the positive emotions I experience. If the other person doesn't respond as I expect, I am quick to judge them and react negatively, even though they never asked to participate in my little feel-good exercise. Yet, for all I know, they could simply be deep in thought or rushing somewhere and not in a frame of mind to appreciate or even notice my gesture.

Your results

How did you do on the generosity test? I imagine you're probably the kind of person that already holds the door open for others. But what are you *thinking* when you do so? What are you *expecting*? Your intentions and expectations will determine how you feel about making the gesture and how the other person responds.

As you offer contributions to your network, you will need to do so without any strings attached. That takes practice. Start now with one of the simplest contributions you can make.

EXERCISE: Your first contribution (10 minutes)

Your first contribution is to give something that everyone has to offer: attention. Start by searching the internet (or your intranet at work) for each individual on your relationship list, looking for some kind of online presence they may have, such as a Twitter account, a blog, an intranet profile, or some online content they've created.

For example, if you both have a Twitter account or intranet profile, follow them there. If they publish on LinkedIn or the intranet or have their own website, start reading, and if you like what you find, let them know by hitting a Like button. If you want to keep receiving updates, look for a Follow button or the ability to subscribe by email.

You don't have to write a comment or message. This first contribution is just a small, unobtrusive signal to the other person. If you don't already know each other, it moves the relationship from "the person doesn't know I exist" to "they may have seen my name." For people you do know, even those you know well, pressing a Follow or Like button is a signal to them that "I see you" and "I care about what you have to say."

Update your relationship list now (or add to your original list on page 157). For each person on your list, include where you found and offered attention to them. (If you don't find an online presence for someone, simply write "Nothing yet.")

1 _____ _____

2 _____ _____

3 _____ _____

4 _____ _____

5 _____ _____

6 _____ _____

7 _____ _____

8 _____ _____

9 _____ _____

10 _____ _____

Q: Is that it? How will this help me?

The like or follow you offered in this exercise is just a first step. On its own, it may not change much. But over time there is a cumulative effect. With each contribution you make, you deepen the sense of relatedness with someone, and gradually build trust. That's what increases the chances of the two of you exchanging information, earning you access to knowledge, people, and opportunities.

During the rest of your guided mastery program, you'll learn about making contributions that take more effort but may have more value. You'll practice generosity with more people in a wider variety of contexts and discover other gifts you have to offer.

"Annoy me with praise!"

What's something that's free, fun, and feels so good you'll want more of it? Something we all don't get enough of?

It's appreciation. (That's what you guessed, isn't it?) A poignant story from business writer Scott Berkun helped me better understand how everyone values the simple gift of appreciation and why we consistently fail to give it. Berkun worked at Microsoft before moving on to become a popular author and speaker. Here's an excerpt from an essay he wrote, describing an exchange he had with a colleague as he was about to leave. It contains so many good points that I've included three entire paragraphs.[1]

On my last day at Microsoft I was invited to do a last lecture. It was a wonderful event and I talked about important things to a friendly crowd. Afterwards, a peer I respected but didn't know walked my way. He thanked me for the work I'd done. I asked why he'd never said anything before. He told me (get this) he thought I already knew. He figured I probably heard that sort of thing all the time. In essence, he didn't want to annoy me with praise. Annoy me with praise! Is there a more absurd phrase in the English language?

It made me think how many times I'd seen or read things that mattered to me and how rare it was I'd offered any praise in return. Books that I loved (or read dozens of times), lectures I enjoyed, good advice I'd received, that I'd never thanked the person for. Or never made an effort to champion their work to others. Dozens of people who said honest things that changed me for the better, or who stuck up for me when others didn't, who never learned the value their words had. I recognized an infinity of actions that made a difference to me that I had not acknowledged in any way and I was poisoned by it. I was less than the man who'd thanked me on my way out of the company. He did something about what mattered to him. He walked straight up, looked me in the eye, and offered his thanks, something, I realized, I didn't know how to do.

These little forgotten things, a short e-mail, a comment on a website, a handshake and a thank you, were not things I'd ever learned. And I realized, in my twisted little attic of a mind, in a hidden dark corner covered in dust, was the belief that offering praise in those contexts was a lessening of my self-opinion. That to compliment was to admit a kind of failure in myself: an association between those kinds of praise and sycophancy. I know now what a fool I've been, for it takes a better man to acknowledge goodness in others than it does to merely be *good oneself. Anyone can criticize or accept praise, but initiating a positive exchange is a hallmark of a difference maker.*

I was struck by Berkun's observations that these "little forgotten things" are so important—and that offering them is something you can practice until it feels natural and becomes a habit.

EXERCISE: Another universal gift (10 minutes)

The next universal gift you'll offer is *gratitude* or *appreciation*. Think of two people you would like to thank for something they have done or said. It can be something recent or it can be recalling an event in the past that comes to mind. One message will be private, a short text or email that says something like, "I was thinking of you and what you did for me, and I wanted to say how much I appreciated it." Everyone would love to get such a note. The other thank-you will be public, @-mentioning them on a platform like LinkedIn or Twitter, in an online community, or on your social intranet at work.

Take the next ten minutes to reflect on what you would like to offer and how you'll offer it. Then send both messages now.

	NAME	MESSAGE
PRIVATE MESSAGE		
PUBLIC MESSAGE		

Q: I'm not sure what to say.

There's a reason many of us buy a Mother's Day card on Mother's Day. The date on the calendar offers us a trigger or reminder to act, and the pre-printed card captures a sentiment we would like to express. When we don't have a trigger or feel we don't have the right words, we too often miss the chance to communicate our appreciation.

Consider the exercise in this chapter as the trigger, and think of these kinds of contributions as signals to the other person that show your interest in them in an unobtrusive, positive way. If you're unsure of the words to use, start with a short personal message, maybe only a sentence or two.

"I was thinking of you today because . . ."
"Thank you so much for . . ."
"I really appreciate the way you . . ."

As an example, here's a small contribution I made to Austin Kleon, author of several best-selling books and a wonderful newsletter, which I shared on Twitter as a token of my appreciation for his work.

Q: It doesn't feel right. It's... uncomfortable.

When you're feeling this kind of discomfort, use it as a trigger to examine your intentions. Is it uncomfortable because you're not being genuine, or because you're simply unused to offering appreciation? The more you practice offering gestures of appreciation without expectations, the more comfortable it will feel. If it ever feels fake or inauthentic, don't do it.

Q: I offered gratitude to someone and they didn't say anything. What did I do wrong?

It's human to want to be acknowledged for what you do. But remember the generosity test: real gifts don't have strings attached. Besides, you have no idea *why* they didn't respond. The other person may be busy or may not have seen your message. With practice, you'll learn to avoid making up negative stories when someone doesn't respond, and focus instead on the next contribution. We'll explore this further in chapter 18.

Reciprocity—for better and for worse

There's a dark side to gift-giving, which is manipulation. In Robert Cialdini's oft-cited book *Influence*, he writes about how people are wired to reciprocate and how you can use that to influence them to do things. Charities, for example, often include a small token like address labels in their mailed requests for a donation. That triggers a sense of obligation and makes it more likely you'll do something in return.

It works. Even a social media–savvy person like Guy Kawasaki included a reference to Cialdini's work in his book, *Enchantment*, advising you to "invoke reciprocity":[2]

When you help someone with something, and they say thank you, say "I know you would do the same for me." Most people would then be obligated to return the favor at this point.

But how does that *feel*? Does it produce sustainable results, or does it work only once? After you receive the first batch of free address labels or see an overt mention of returning the favor, you get the idea that you're being manipulated, or that the other person is keeping score.

A better approach to giving

Do you remember Reid Hoffman's "theory of small gifts" from chapter 6? It was from an article titled "Connections with Integrity," and in this context it offers advice that's very different from "invoking reciprocity":[3]

It seems counterintuitive, but the more altruistic your attitude, the more benefits you will gain from the relationship. If you insist on a quid pro quo every time you help others, you will have a much narrower network and a more limited set of opportunities. Conversely, if you set out to help others ... simply because you think it's the right thing to do, you will rapidly reinforce your own reputation and expand your universe of possibilities.

Small gifts, freely given, are like magic for both parties. For the giver, the contributions feel authentic and genuine because there are no strings attached. It's easier to give because you're not manipulating or promoting, you're being helpful. The receiver, sensing this, isn't burdened by the weight of an obligation, and the gift no longer feels like an unwanted transaction.

You experience benefits from making contributions, but it isn't necessarily on an individual basis—"I did this for you, and you'll pay me back." *It's over the course of your network*. Across the set of relationships in your network, the tendency to reciprocate will yield an aggregate benefit for you, and eliminate the need to keep score.

Offering small gifts freely takes practice. That's why there are so many contribution exercises in this part of the book. The repeated practice will help you develop new habits and a new mindset regarding how you make contributions. Your small gifts, freely given over the course of your network, will deepen relationships and unlock access to possibilities.

KEY IDEAS IN THIS CHAPTER

- An offer of attention, like following someone online, can move a relationship from "the person doesn't know I exist" to "they may have seen my name."

- For someone you already know, pressing a Follow or Like button can signal that "I see you" and "I care about what you have to say."

- Honest and sincere appreciation is a simple but powerful universal gift. It is something everyone can offer and everyone likes to receive.

- If you think people you admire may not value your recognition, think of Scott Berkun's story about the value of the "little forgotten things." *Annoy them with praise!*

- Remember the generosity test. What are you thinking when you make a contribution? What are you expecting? Intention makes all the difference in how it feels to offer or receive a gift.

EXERCISES

Something you can do in less than a minute
Think of the last time someone showed appreciation for something you did. How did you feel? How do you think they felt in offering it to you?

Something you can do in less than 5 minutes
Another simple way to show attention and appreciation is by commenting on someone's blog or LinkedIn post. Here's an example. In this chapter I referred to Scott Berkun's blog post, and I enjoyed it so much that I shared it with my network via Twitter, just as you offered appreciation in one of the exercises in this chapter. The tweet was easy to write and was quickly retweeted by a friend.

But I felt I wanted to do more, so I decided to comment on his post on his website as well. That took longer to write, perhaps three or four minutes, but it felt more personal, so the extra time was worth it to me. Much to my surprise, Scott replied the same day.

Skim through your LinkedIn feed, or through blogs that you follow, and post a comment now.

John Stepper
@johnstepper

Follow

Love this by @berkun on showing appreciation, etc: "These little forgotten things..were not things I'd ever learned." scottberkun.com/essays/49-how- ...

3:09 PM - 2 Jun 2014

1 Retweet

JOHN STEPPER | JUNE 2

I loved this post. I first read it last month in "Mindfire" and then came back to it here. Since then, I've retold your story and used "Annoy me with praise!" to show how rarely we offer the universal gifts of appreciation and recognition. I hope to use the story in a book I'm writing called "Working Out Loud."

One particular line struck me. "These little forgotten things...were not things I'd ever learned." I think the general lack of appreciation we experience isn't due to some flaw in our make-up or some sinister reasoning but simply ignorance: most people don't know how to do it. And even those who do tend not to have a method or practice for doing it consistently.

Those are easier problems to solve. And that gives me hope.

I know you wrote this 6 years ago, but I'll take the risk of annoying you with praise and say thanks again for a great post :-)

SCOTT | JUNE 2

Thanks John. As corny as it sounds, I reread this essay now and then as I know I forget to take its advice. Many of these philosophical essays are/were written to help me remind myself of things I forget.

12

Take Three Small Steps

*Small steps may appear unimpressive,
but don't be deceived. They are the means by
which perspectives are subtly altered, mountains are
gradually scaled, and lives are drastically changed.*

RICHELLE E. GOODRICH, *Making Wishes*

SO FAR, WORKING OUT LOUD may seem conceptually simple. You think of a few people related to your goal. You click on a Like or Follow button, say some nice things. What's all the fuss about?

The challenge, as with almost any new habit, is to keep practicing in such a way that you become more effective and the new behavior feels more natural, even automatic. This chapter will help you to keep making progress by taking three small steps.

Investing in yourself

One of the biggest barriers to developing yourself and your career—and one of the themes of modern life—is being busy. Most people don't have the time to do the things they know would be good for them, whether that's exercising or eating right or (ahem) doing the exercises in this book.

I found a cure for this problem in a book called *The Richest Man in Babylon*.[1] When a smart, successful person recommended it to me I was expecting well-crafted historical fiction, or perhaps some stimulating anthropology. Instead it was a seventy-one-page, poorly typeset pamphlet from 1926 about "thrift and financial success, using parables set in Babylon." The author, George Clason, owned a map company in Colorado when he wrote it, and banks and insurance companies distributed his pamphlet to help customers learn how to manage their money. Despite its humble appearance and purpose, this simple guide for managing money held valuable lessons for managing other important resources, including time.

The richest man in Babylon's first and most important lesson is to set aside 10 percent of your money before spending anything. "A part of all you earn is yours to keep. It should not be less than a tenth no matter how little you earn . . . Pay yourself first."

It seemed obvious that I should use the same approach with time, and yet I hadn't. Although I knew it would be better for me and the company I worked for if I invested in developing my skills, I instead allowed my calendar to fill up with appointments created by other people, or I frittered away what little free time I had with low-value activities. Like the majority of the people in Babylon, I spent a precious resource unwisely and was all the poorer for it.

EXERCISE: Pay yourself first (5 minutes)

Right now, "pay yourself first" by taking a look at your calendar and scheduling appointments over the next month for doing something related to your goal, such as doing the exercises in this book, or reviewing the activity of people on your relationship list. You might block out one hour a week, or make several shorter appointments. Even one regular fifteen-minute slot while you have coffee can make a meaningful difference.

Make at least four appointments with yourself over the next four weeks, and update your calendar now.

Q: I want to invest in myself, but I really don't have time.

Though we all have different jobs and different schedules, very few people feel they have extra time. After all, your time is already accounted for, so when you choose to do something new you have to make a trade of some kind. For example, whenever you say yes to a meeting or a task, you're saying no to something else that could be much more valuable. Ask yourself, "What's the something else?"

Even in 1926, George Clason recognized in his pamphlet that "what each of us calls our 'necessary expenses' will always grow to equal our incomes unless we protest to the contrary." Since your time is most likely fully allocated, you probably won't find *spare* time. But you can identify activities you'll start saying no to, so you can invest in things more important to you in the long term.

The richest man in Babylon also advises to "guard thy treasures from loss" and to avoid wasteful ventures. You can't make extra time, but you can make more mindful decisions about how you spend the time you have. This exercise is aimed at helping you exchange low-value activities for a bit more time to invest in yourself.

Q: There's no way I can find time in my schedule. Now what?

I completely understand. If you feel like you already have a full week, finding an hour can be daunting. Here are a few things you might do. (These are just a few techniques for helping you practice and make progress. We'll explore more ideas in chapter 19, "Making It a Habit.")

- Check that your goal is something you care about. The more you care about it, the more motivated you'll be to find time to work on it.

- If one hour a week is too much, try half an hour. If that's too much, try two fifteen-minute increments. Just be sure to schedule them. Touching the treadmill can help you get started.

- If you're still struggling, keep a time journal for a week and track how you're spending time. Review it at the end of each day and ask what the richest man in Babylon might say. Did you pay yourself first? Did you invest your time wisely? The point isn't to criticize yourself for wasting time, but instead to help you make more conscious choices about how you use the time available to you. I did this exercise myself when I thought I didn't have enough time to work on this book, and after a few days it became clear I was spending more time on my phone—checking Facebook and meandering on the internet—than I had thought. I cut back on that and invested that time in writing.

- If you can't find time in the next few weeks, look further out. Chances are that your calendar is relatively empty three months from now. Schedule a recurring meeting with yourself then, and when the time comes, you'll have already reserved oases of self-development in your weeks and months.

Extending your reach

In one of my first Circles, a friend complained that she wasn't able to find many people related to her goal. I sat next to her, opened up my laptop, and started to search using keywords she gave me. Within a few minutes we found several online communities, authors, speakers, videos, and other resources. My friend was surprised and a bit irritated that it was so easy. "What did you do?" she asked me, as if I had used some secret googling technique. "I swear those results weren't there before."

I since learned this kind of thing happens quite often. Although most people are familiar with browsing the internet, we're not necessarily used to playing internet detective, following up on clues and coming up with different ways to look at the problem. As a result, our lists of possible connections are much smaller than they could be, limiting our exploration.

One way to accelerate developing your network is to leverage networks that already exist. Think of it as searching for places where people related to your goal are already congregating. When you land on such a place, you can readily find hundreds or even thousands of individuals who might be suitable for your relationship list. And when you make a contribution to a group instead of an individual, you can become visible to many people in that group, further extending your reach.

Contributing to one or more of these networks isn't a replacement for deepening individual relationships. It's just a way to come into contact with more people, knowledge, and possibilities. Here are some suggestions for different kinds of networks that might improve your online sleuthing.

Communities at work or on the internet

These are usually formed by people who are passionate about a particular topic and want to help others learn more about it. Joining such a group—whether it's online or in person—is an extremely efficient and effective way to find people related to something you care about. Whether the community is related to a skill, a role, an interest, or a hobby, you'll find a vast array of online groups that are eager to have new members and more contributions.

Groups that offer related products or services

Examples include product vendors and professional organizations. If you want to become a better project manager, say, then look for organizations offering training or tools related to project management.

Conferences and meet-ups

This is where people related to your goal will congregate in person. Organizers are often eager for contributions—from help promoting the events to volunteering to presenting stories and projects. Even if you don't attend the event, you can easily find people who have attended by searching the internet for the event's hashtag. For example, if your goal is related to knowledge management, and you discovered the APQC Knowledge Management Conference while playing internet detective, then searching the event hashtag #APQCKM will lead you to people who are posting content about the event and the topic.

Influential individuals

Look through your relationship list and identify people in your network who have much more influence than others on the list. If you don't find anyone, you might start by looking for people who are already reaching an online audience, such as bloggers, authors of books and articles, and other content providers related to your goal. Their audience is a rich source of possible connections for your relationship list.

EXERCISE: Leveraging existing networks (15 minutes)
Play internet or intranet detective and find at least five online groups or communities that are relevant to your goal.

1 _____

2 _____

3 _____

4 _____

5 _____

If you're stuck, join one of these two WOL communities and explore:

- Facebook: facebook.com/groups/workingoutloud
- LinkedIn: linkedin.com/groups/4937010

Who's there? What are they talking about? If you make a contribution of attention—even a simple "Hello, I'm reading *Working Out Loud* and I'm interested in learning more"—it will evoke responses from around the world.

A fundamental human skill

The third small step in this chapter is to make another contribution, another small signal that can deepen the feeling of relatedness between you and another person.

Why would an exchange of simple signals make a difference in relationships? In *The Culture Code: The Secrets of Highly Successful Groups*,[2] author Daniel Coyle asserts that the cultures of the world's most successful groups "are created by a specific set of skills which tap into the power of our social brains." The first of these skills is to "build safety," learning how to exchange signals that build social bonds of belonging and identity. These signals, or "belonging cues," as Coyle calls them, communicate three things:

1 I see you.
2 I care about you.
3 We have a shared future together.

When we exchange these signals, we feel accepted and psychologically safe. When we don't, we feel uncertain and increasingly anxious. The phrase "psychological safety" may seem more suitable for the laboratory than the workplace or home, but when Google analyzed teams to discover what set successful ones apart from others, they found that psychological safety is "far and away the most important."[3] The less safe you feel, the less likely you are to say or do something—such as make a suggestion or admit a mistake—that might possibly result in a conflict or loss of status. A reluctance to contribute is bad for the individual and bad for the team.

The belonging cues are so important they're even taught in elementary schools. Here's how the Professional Learning Board describes the SLANT strategy:[4]

"SLANT" is an acronym that stands for "Sit up, Lean forward, Ask and answers questions, Nod your head and Track the speaker." It is a simple technique to encourage and remind students on being attentive and active in class. The crux of the SLANT strategy is to enhance learning and student performance by creating a behavior incorporating the conscious use of positive body language.

Track the speaker and make eye contact. *I see you.* Nod your head. *I care about what you have to say.* Ask and answer questions. *We have a shared future together.* Exchanging signals in a way that leads to better communication and collaboration, as well as healthier work environments and cultures, is a learnable skill. It can also be simple, as you'll see in the next exercise.

EXERCISE: Intimacy with a stranger (5 minutes)

Recently, I heard Daniel Coyle speak at a conference in Houston. He's an insightful, intelligent, engaging presenter —and I had to give a talk after him! In my presentation, I compared the exchanges of signals that he had talked about to the giving and receiving that takes place as you Work Out Loud. In my workshop after the talk, I included an exercise on offering a contribution of appreciation, and a woman in the audience demonstrated how easy it can be to communicate belonging cues.

Sarah Crass
@SarahCrass

Follow

I am Working Out Loud with @johnstepper here at #APQCKM #WOL - I'm totally taking this back to @WorldVision #WorkOutLoud

2:45 PM - 2 May 2019

With a single sentence, Sarah Crass made it clear she was listening to what I had to say, was interested in it, and expected to use it in the future. Writing her tweet took just a few seconds, and it led to a further exchange during the workshop.

If it's so easy, why don't we have more successful groups and positive cultures? Why don't we establish connections more readily? Because the hard part—the art of communications and good relationships—is to practice making these exchanges over and over again, reinforcing and enhancing social bonds. That's the thing most of us struggle with. We forget to say what we feel, we avoid the risk of discomfort, or we assume the other person knows.

Try it yourself now, using Sarah Crass's tweet as an example. Look for someone on your relationship list or whom you otherwise admire, and offer the three belonging cues privately via text or email or publicly via a social network.

The heart of your WOL practice

Ten thousand years ago, you would die if you were rejected by your social group—and we still carry an instinctual need for belonging deep in our brains. It may no longer be life or death, but we feel pain when we sense we're being rejected, and we feel good when we sense we're accepted and safe. Over millennia, to improve our collective chances of belonging and surviving, human beings evolved highly sophisticated ways of tracking the status of group members in ways that help us cooperate and collaborate.

The basis of human connection is an exchange of signals. Though you're just getting started with Working Out Loud, developing the habit of offering attention and appreciation will change how you relate to people and how they relate to you. If this is all you get from this book, that will be enough. Yet there are many more contributions you can make and signals you can send, and you'll practice the next set of them in the following section, Connecting.

KEY IDEAS IN THIS CHAPTER

- One of the biggest barriers to developing yourself and your career is being busy. Think of time as a valuable resource and remember to *pay yourself first*, looking for ways to trade your lowest value activities for others that will benefit you in the long term.

- A way to accelerate developing your network is to search for places where people related to your goal are already congregating, such as online communities. That's a way to discover more people for your relationship list, and also to amplify the effects of any contributions you might make.

- At the heart of WOL is the human exchange of signals that build social bonds of belonging and identity. These signals, or belonging cues, communicate *I see you; I care about you; we have a shared future together*. When we exchange these signals, we feel safe and accepted. When we don't, we feel uncertain and increasingly anxious.

EXERCISES

Something you can do in less than a minute

A study comparing an individual's estimate of their smartphone usage with their actual usage showed that "actual uses amounted to more than double the estimated number," and that "people have little awareness of the frequency with which they check their phone."[5]

Take a minute to reflect on your own phone usage. Do you think you are making a conscious choice or simply reacting? Are you paying yourself first?

Something you can do in less than 5 minutes

It was such a short, simple exchange and yet it left an impression on me. I was sitting in a crowded food court at lunchtime, working on my laptop. There was the usual din of people eating, laughing, shuffling chairs. Amidst all of the office workers, I noticed someone on the maintenance staff wiping down tables after people left, getting them ready for the next group.

When he cleaned the table next to me, I offered my appreciation for what he was doing. He nodded, smiled awkwardly, and kept wiping the table. A few seconds later he walked by me, leaned in, eyes averted, and quietly said, "Thank you for saying that." I think it was the earnestness in his voice that struck me. It was as if my simple comment was something especially valuable to him, something rare.

Today, as you see someone you would normally pass by, offer them attention or appreciation by greeting them or thanking them for their work. Perhaps it's the person cleaning the restroom, doing the landscaping, or providing some other service we tend to take for granted. As you make your contribution, pay special attention to how you feel. Notice the expression on the other person's face and imagine how they might be feeling.

- [x] GETTING STARTED
- [x] **CONNECTING**
- [ ] CREATING
- [ ] LEADING

13

How to Approach People

*If out of this book you get just one thing—
an increased tendency to think always in terms of
other people's point of view, and see things
from their angle—if you get that one thing
out of this book, it may easily prove to be one of
the building blocks of your career.*

DALE CARNEGIE, *How to Win Friends and Influence People*

IT HAPPENED DURING a trip to New Orleans when I was
in my early twenties. Though I grew up in New York City,
I wasn't particularly street smart or used to traveling. So
when a man approached me and complimented me on my
sneakers, I stopped and thanked him. I remember feeling proud that the fine footwear I was sporting attracted
the attention of the good people of New Orleans. That
moment of hesitation was all it took. Next thing I know,
he got down on one knee, spit on my sneaker, and started

vigorously buffing it with a rag. I was embarrassed at his generosity until he demanded twenty dollars. Reciprocal altruism, indeed! I gave him ten bucks and walked away with a healthy suspicion of strangers offering gifts.

How your contribution will be received depends on how well you know the person and how you present the gift, no matter whether you're presenting it in person, via email, or on social media. Even asking for help can be framed as a contribution if you know how. This chapter provides you with guidance for how to approach people, and exercises to help you practice.

EXERCISE: Intimacy levels (3 minutes)

When you offer a contribution to someone, it helps to be mindful that relationships in your network differ in terms of the depth of the connection. For example, the email you send to a friend asking for help should be different from the request you send to a complete stranger. Yet as obvious as that is, we often get it wrong. Our approach to a trusted friend or colleague may feel impersonal, or our initial outreach to someone we don't know can come off as invasive instead of friendly.

To help you be mindful of the different levels of intimacy, here's a simple scale from one to five:

1 The person doesn't know you exist.
2 You're connected in some way (for example, you follow them online).
3 You've had one or more interactions.

4 You've collaborated, even in a small way.
5 You regularly interact, exchange ideas, and help each other.

For this quick exercise, go through your relationship list on page 157 and jot down your intimacy level for each person. As you do, keep in mind that the objective isn't to get to level five with everyone. You're just trying to deepen some of your relationships, and to do so with contributions that are appropriate given the level of trust and intimacy you share with a particular person.

Three questions to help you

We're wired to quickly calculate whether reciprocal altruism will turn a contribution into a debt we don't want to incur. If you offer contributions that feel like too much too soon, you're more likely to evoke suspicion instead of gratitude. *Who is this person? What does he want from me?*

The following three questions can help you improve both what you offer and how you offer it:

1 What would my reaction be if I were that person?
2 Why should they care?
3 Why am I doing this?

The first question invokes empathy, making you more mindful of the words you use. The second helps you focus on the value to the recipient instead of the value to you. The third question helps you examine your motives and gives you the chance to rethink them if necessary. Combined, the three questions can improve the tone of your communications. When you take the other person's perspective, and frame your contribution as a genuine gift, it liberates you from the fear of being pushy or being rejected. Examining your motives also helps you avoid being manipulative or insincere, or otherwise doing something you're uncomfortable with.

Seth Godin describes the tone of effective outreach as "the sound of confidence," where your approach is characterized by "Generosity, not arrogance. Problem-solving, not desperation. Helpfulness, not selfishness."[1] If you're generous and helpful as you approach someone, you'll feel much more comfortable than if you're arrogant, desperate, and selfish. This concept might seem obvious to you, but in practice people routinely come across as arrogant, desperate, and selfish, usually without even knowing it.

Here are exercises that can increase the chances your gift is well-received. You can think of them as ways to further develop your own sense of empathy in different contexts with different kinds of people.

EXERCISE: The inbox empathy game (10 minutes)
You can find examples of empathy—and the lack of it—in your email inbox. The inspiration for this exercise appeared more than eighty years ago in *How to Win Friends and Influence People:*[2]

If there is any one secret of success, it lies in the ability to get the other person's point of view and see things from that person's angle as well as from your own. That is so simple, so obvious, that anyone ought to see the truth of it at a glance; yet 90 percent of the people on this earth ignore it 90 percent of the time. An example? Look at the letters that come across your desk tomorrow morning, and you will find that most of them violate this important canon of common sense.

For example, here's an actual message I received from a professional salesperson. How would you feel if you got a message like this? Eager to respond or a bit irritated?

Did you get my last email? I wanted to follow up on a couple of attempts to connect with you.

Take a look at these next real examples. How you would feel if you received these messages? What is the lack of empathy in each one?

ACTUAL EMAIL TEXT	LACK OF EMPATHY
"I'd love to take you to lunch and pick your brain. Any chance you're free one day over the next two weeks?"	
"Do you have time to talk or meet up? I would value the opportunity for a twenty-minute meeting."	
"Let me know, as I have some time over the next few days."	

Messages like these are common. People frequently offer to pick your brain or invoke reciprocity by buying you coffee in exchange for information. They're not bad people and those aren't terrible things to do. It's just that the senders could elicit a better response if they took a bit more time to think of how the other person feels when reading their message. That's empathy. If the people who sent me the above messages had asked themselves those three questions, they would have written their emails differently and increased the chances of a positive response.

Take a look at your own inbox now. Look for messages or phrases that irritate you or otherwise show a lack of empathy, and write down the reasons why you picked them. Try to come up with five examples. These will be useful in the next exercise.

EXAMPLE	LACK OF EMPATHY

Q: Why do you keep emphasizing empathy?

For sharing to feel like a contribution, you need to practice, and the best tool or technique is empathy: *What will the other person be thinking as she reads this?* Having this thought in mind will help you craft messages that are more likely to be read and appreciated. In *How to Win Friends and Influence People*, Dale Carnegie quotes twentieth-century industrialist Owen D. Young: "People who can put themselves in the place of other people, who can understand the workings of their minds, need never worry about what the future has in store for them."

EXERCISE: Earn someone else's attention
(10 minutes)

The point of the previous exercise was not to criticize others, but instead to help you fine-tune your own sense of what makes for ineffective communications, and to consider how they might be improved. Now you can put that sense to use.

In this exercise, you'll practice offering another kind of simple contribution: sharing a resource that you've found interesting or useful. Your message needn't be long, but it should be personal and authentic. You'll want your messages to include these three elements:

1 *Appreciation:* Demonstrate that you've paid attention to the recipient.
2 *Context:* Mention why you thought of the recipient specifically in relation to what you're sharing.

3 *Value:* Describe the potential benefit to the recipient.

Let's say I came across some content that I found really useful, and I thought of someone else who might also find it useful. First, I put myself in the other person's shoes as I'm writing my message, and I anticipate the questions they might have: *Who is this person? Why are they sending this to me? What am I supposed to do with it?* Here's an example:

Subject: Three press releases you might find useful

Hi, Lisa.

I saw your tweet about starting a WOL Circle in your organization. That's excellent!

I thought you might find these press releases helpful. The first two are from Bosch, a global company with 400,000 people that is spreading WOL. One is about why they spread it. One is an interview about WOL with a board member responsible for HR. The last one is from Daimler and has a great quote from the head of the Works Council there.

These articles can be good to share at work if you're ever asked about how and why Working Out Loud benefits the company.

http://www.bosch-presse.de/pressportal/de/en/the -future-of-work-virtual-expert-networks-boost-effective ness-135872.html

*http://www.bosch-presse.de/pressportal/de/en/working
-out-loud-at-bosch-137280.html*

*https://media.daimler.com/marsMediaSite/en/instance/
ko/DigitalLifeaDaimler-transformation-of-the-working
-world-Daimler-and-Bosch-hold-the-first-inter-company
-Working-Out-Loud-conference.xhtml?oid=41686666*

*Have a great week!
John*

Now it's your turn. Choose an article, book, video, TED talk, or other resource you would like to share, and write it down here.

_____

Next, ask yourself, "For whom might this be a contribution?" Try to list three people.

_____

_____

_____

The last step is to share the resource you picked with at least one of the three people you listed, using any platform you prefer—email, text, Twitter, Facebook, or LinkedIn. The less intimate the relationship, the less invasive the channel you should use. For example, @-mentions on Twitter or your corporate intranet are neither an intrusion nor a burden, whereas a text message can be seen as both. (Email is in between the two.)

Q: No offense, but I think your letter is terrible.

Great! That means you're attuning your attention to what makes for effective communications. Maybe you think it's too long? Or the way I wrote it seems insincere or self-serving? Or three links is too many? Use those opinions to improve your own messages.

Q: I assumed Working Out Loud involves using social media, but these exercises refer to email a lot. Why?

Working Out Loud doesn't *require* you to use social media. You can use traditional channels—even talking over coffee—to share your work in a way that helps others. But email is still the predominant means of communication in most organizations, and is well-suited for sharing something in a personalized way with a specific individual.

There are benefits to using social platforms, where sharing your work amplifies who you are and what you do, extends your reach, and expands your set of contributions and how you can offer them. But if, for any reason, you don't want to use social media, start by using what you're comfortable with. That way you're more likely to make progress.

Q: It feels fake.

If it feels fake or inauthentic, stop. Only offer genuine gifts. For example, don't pretend to share a useful resource if you didn't find it truly useful. Also, remember not to worry about a response. It's often the expectation of getting something in return that can spoil a gift.

Offering contributions should make you feel good. If you don't have positive feelings as you're making contributions to people on your relationship list, reflect on both what you're offering and how you're offering it.

A source of resistance and how to overcome it

I remember sitting in a room of senior managers responsible for the IT department where I worked, talking with them about the new collaboration platform I had introduced. The software displayed a small text box where you could share something, just like the exercise above, and all the managers agreed it was a good way for employees to share knowledge, as well as a good way for leaders to communicate. Yet not a single one of them used it. Why not?

One manager I knew well, who was responsible for a hundred-million-dollar budget and a large staff, told me, "I'm not sure what to say." Though he was a smart, confident executive, that slight self-doubt was all it took to prevent him from doing something he knew would be good for him, his organization, and the company.

The ancient parts of our brain are constantly trying to protect us from possible threats, and sharing something is akin to stepping out into the savannah. You feel exposed. *What if I say something stupid? What if they don't like it?* The safe thing to do is to do nothing, but that's a lose-lose situation. You miss out on a chance to connect with other people, and other people miss out on the contributions you could have made.

If you're worried that your contribution isn't good enough, remember that, at this point in your Working Out Loud practice, you're focusing on offering small gifts. This isn't a high-risk activity. Even if someone doesn't love what you share, they will appreciate your thoughtfulness and attention if you share it in a personal, authentic way. The value of a gift often has more to do with how it is offered than the worth of the thing itself. Also, remember the generosity test from chapter 11. When you make a genuine contribution without expectations, it makes it easier for you to give and for others to receive.

The more you practice, the more comfortable you'll become making a range of contributions. In the next chapter, you'll see how even small steps can lead to purposeful outcomes and make bigger steps possible.

KEY IDEAS IN THIS CHAPTER

- Some relationships in your network will be more intimate and meaningful than others. How your contribution will be received depends on how well you know the person and how you present the gift, no matter whether you're presenting it in person, via email, or on Twitter.

- Practicing empathy and being mindful of your own intentions are the most important things to do when you approach someone. *What would my reaction be if I were that person? Why should they care? Why am I doing this?*

- When you share a resource you find useful or interesting, include Appreciation, Context, and Value in your message. That helps the other person understand why you're sending it and why you thought of them specifically. It makes it easier for them to receive your gift.

- Self-doubt can make you feel that the safe thing to do is nothing, but then you miss an opportunity to connect with other people, and others miss out on the contributions you could have made.

- Even if someone doesn't love what you share, they will appreciate your thoughtfulness and attention if you share it in a personal, authentic way.

EXERCISES

Something you can do in less than a minute

Think of a message you received recently that made you feel more connected to the person who sent it. What was it about the message that made you feel that way? Try to identify how you could use some of those same elements to make others feel more connected to you, and to make your messages more personal and engaging.

Something you can do in less than 5 minutes

Here's another empathy exercise: Imagine you receive a LinkedIn connection request from someone with the default, impersonal message provided by LinkedIn:

I'd like to join your LinkedIn network.

How would you feel? If you're like me, you might think, "Gee, he couldn't even spend thirty seconds to send a personal message!" Requesting a LinkedIn connection provides an opportunity to practice empathy. You should *always* personalize your request.

Now pick someone in your network with whom you've interacted already and send him or her a personal request. If you're still unsure, you can send me a request and put in a personal greeting. (You might mention that you're reading this book or tell me which part you found helpful. I am purposefully not including a sample message since I want you to write your own.)

Some of you may find that LinkedIn makes it difficult to send a personalized request, particularly from your phone. Search the internet for instructions or ask a friend for help. Or, if you fail to send a personalized invitation, try to follow up with an email to explain why you want to connect. Your personalized note will stand out amid all the generic, computer-generated requests that people receive, so it's worth the time to do it well.

14

Deepening Relationships Through Contribution

The fact that I'm me and no one else is one of my greatest assets.

HARUKI MURAKAMI,
What I Talk About When I Talk About Running

DO YOU REMEMBER Mara, the woman in chapter 1 with "the worst job possible" configuring Lotus Notes databases? By Working Out Loud, she discovered other people and other projects, and wound up creating a new kind of job at her company. A few years later, she had a different purpose: she wanted to go home. Mara had spent a large part of her life in New Zealand and much of her family was still there. She had come to London for work and enjoyed the city, but she missed the natural beauty of New Zealand and thought the schools there would be better for her children. The problem was finding a job.

"Do you think the company would relocate me?" she asked me.

Maybe. However, there were only a few dozen employees in the New Zealand office, so the odds were slim. "But Mara," I said, "there are four and a half million people in the country. You'll have a much better shot if you look outside the company too."

In effect, Mara would be buying career insurance by doing so. If all she did was wait for an approval from her managers and the office in New Zealand, she would be leaving her fate in the hands of others. But by purposefully exploring a range of possibilities that would be better for her and her family, she would create options in case she didn't get the answer she wanted. That gave her more control and less anxiety.

Starting to make more significant contributions

Mara did all the things that you did in the Getting Started section. She wrote down her goal and drew up a relationship list. She played internet detective and started following people and liking things.

"Now what?" she asked me.

What transpired next is an example of what can happen to you when you develop the habit of making small contributions. One of the people on Mara's list was the CEO of a large company in New Zealand. Mara liked what the company did and saw that the CEO was active on Twitter, so she followed him. Then she read his posts and occasionally retweeted some of them or offered appreciation, and at one point the CEO replied with a simple "thank you."

None of these individual actions took much effort or involved much risk, but Mara had gone from *he doesn't know I exist* to *we've interacted*. Then it got more interesting. In one particular tweet, the CEO posted a complaint about a social platform his firm was using. This was something Mara had ideas and opinions about, so she replied, and he asked her to send him an email with more details. Aha! This would be a different kind of contribution. It would take more thought and more time to write, but it could be more valuable to the CEO and deepen their relationship. She carefully crafted her email so it would be long enough to contain some good ideas, but short enough that he would still read it. He replied, and those emails led to a phone call via Skype and then another call. The calls gave Mara a better understanding of the problems the CEO had, as well as ideas about other contributions she could make. Now she had moved the relationship from *we've interacted* to *we're collaborating*.

Emboldened by these interactions, Mara continued looking for other people related to her goal and ways to contribute, almost always starting with attention and appreciation. She was shocked at her ability to connect with almost everyone and then deepen those relationships. She saw how her expanded network unlocked access to knowledge, experience, other people, and opportunities—all of which would improve the odds of reaching her goal. When one of her contributions led to an exchange with the former prime minister of New Zealand, Mara was exuberant. "It's like magic!"

Practical magic: The five elements

Mara's example illustrates just how easy it can be to reach and engage people when you put the five elements into practice.

Purposeful Discovery: Mara had a goal in mind—find work in New Zealand—that lent itself to exploration and learning. The more she practiced, the more she discovered new people and possibilities.

Relationships: Mara could have broken down her goal into a set of tasks she should execute, but that would assume she knew the path to reach her goal. Instead, the way Mara explored her goal was by building relationships, and it was those connections that showed her different ways to reach her goal, including some she never would have imagined otherwise.

Generosity: When Mara identified someone that might be helpful, she didn't spit on their sneaker by offering things they didn't ask for or want. Instead, she was careful to learn more about them first, offering attention and genuine appreciation. Her mindful generosity is what made it possible to deepen relationships with strangers on the other side of the world.

Visible Work: After offering universal gifts, Mara had the chance to offer something specifically related to her skills and experiences through her email to the CEO. She also ensured her profile and online contributions made it easy for others to see and discover her and her work. (More about how to do that will come in the following chapters.)

A Growth Mindset: Finally, Mara approached the entire process with an open, curious mind. She tried not to worry or get upset if her email wasn't perfect, or the Skype call didn't go well, or if someone didn't respond. She focused on doing the best she could and learning from whatever happened. This mindset is what enabled her to keep taking steps and trying new things, and enjoying both her progress and her personal development.

More important than the specific connections Mara made were the confidence and habits she developed as a result. Over the following months, she built more and more connections inside and outside of the company where we worked, and felt as if she was in control of the process instead of just waiting for a decision. As it turned out, the company did approve her relocation to New Zealand. When she arrived, she already had a strong local network of relationships, and she sent me photos of her family smiling on a beautiful beach.

Of course, not everyone will meet national leaders and CEOs when they Work Out Loud. But you can develop confidence and connections that will take you to surprising places. Here's another example.

Barbara discovers a whole new world

In chapter 10, Barbara was struggling to choose a goal, and finally settled on something she was genuinely interested in related to her hobby.

I want to find other people who share my passion for genealogy and explore possibilities related to that.

To build her network, Barbara began by simply looking for other people like her, including other bloggers, people who organized genealogy conferences, and firms that specialized in family tree research. She followed them online, exchanged emails and tweets, and even had some of her content featured on a popular genealogy website. That's when she discovered that people did genealogy for companies too, and even that her own firm had a corporate historical society. She learned that people made a living producing corporate histories—books, documentaries, and online content. Her favorite example was a beautiful online history for a company in her hometown of Lübeck, and she contacted the person in charge. She discovered that there were associations of archivists across Germany and elsewhere in Europe.

The more Barbara looked, the more she found. In her words, it was like discovering "a whole new world" of possibilities.[1] For the first time, she wondered if she could somehow connect her passion for genealogy to her work inside her company. Perhaps, for example, she could promote the work of the corporate historical society.

She was nervous, though. Sending an email to the director of the historical society felt pushy, and the mere idea of contacting a stranger made her anxious. To help her overcome her self-doubt, she used the approach from the last chapter and wrote a note based on empathy and generosity instead of self-interest. The email was just a few sentences, beginning with Barbara's appreciation for the director's work, and including an offer to help organize an event for the company's historical society if he was interested. She was happy and surprised when she got a response right away, which included a warm thank-you and a request to talk on the phone. Then she wrote to tell me about the call they had.

It was amazing! Again I have this huge grin on my face. He directly asked me for my opinions regarding the examples he sent me and if I have other ideas ... ;-)

"It really works," she wrote me. "And I was so nervous to just approach him unasked." Like with Mara's experience, Barbara's helpful contributions led to more interactions and different ways to contribute and deepen the relationship. She went on to help the historical society organize an event and raise awareness among the company's employees by engaging more people on the enterprise social network. Though she was still looking at complicated spreadsheets, collaborating with the corporate historians helped Barbara feel like she could bring her whole self to work. She also had more control of her learning and her network, and she was routinely discovering new people, ideas, and possibilities in a way that felt purposeful.

A few months later, a senior manager at her firm noticed Barbara's work on the company's intranet and asked if she would join his team. He had never met her, and it wasn't her spreadsheet or genealogy skills that attracted his attention, but the way she communicated and collaborated online. He needed those skills for a new transformation program about to launch that involved reorganizing a big portion of the IT department. They spoke on the phone, and a few weeks later she moved to London to begin a new job and a new phase in her career. "Working Out Loud," Barbara wrote, "changed my life."[2]

Q: But I'm still not sure I picked the right goal. Can I change it?

Yes, you can change it. Many people, after having spent a few weeks thinking about their goal and taking a few steps, discover something that inspires them to make an adjustment. Great! That learning and self-awareness—about what you like and don't like, for example—is all a natural part of the process. It's better to change your goal and enjoy the process than to cling stubbornly to something that doesn't inspire you to do the exercises. Remember that, with practice, you'll develop skills, habits, and a mindset you can apply to any future goal.

Cultivating a sense of relatedness over time

What helped Mara and Barbara make progress toward their goals was that they practiced searching for people related to their goals and reflecting on what they might offer to those people. They had attuned their attention, and they began to see opportunities to connect and contribute that they hadn't considered before.

Notice how it wasn't a single contribution that made a difference for Mara and Barbara. Instead it was a range of different contributions over time that produced a cumulative effect and led to a deepening of some of their relationships. One of those contributions was one that might surprise you.

One more universal gift

Have you ever been in a room of strangers and discovered that someone went to the same school as you? Or grew up in the same hometown? Or has kids the same age? Simply discovering you have a fact in common makes you feel differently about that person. Somehow, you feel you can relate to them better.

Though such occurrences may seem random, you can increase the chances of them happening when you're mindful that many of your own personal facts can deepen a relationship. For example, here are ten facts that, when you share them in the right way, can change how you relate to another person.

Ten possible facts about you
1 Whether you have children, and facts about them.
2 Where you were born.
3 Places you've lived.
4 Where your parents came from.
5 Places you've worked.
6 Vacations you've taken.
7 Physical challenges you've had to deal with.
8 Career challenges you've had.
9 Schools you attended.
10 Things you love doing.

For most of my life I never considered such mundane facts as contributions, if I even thought of them at all. But an incident at work changed that. It happened while I was working on the trading floor of an investment bank, supporting a senior colleague who could be quite gruff and intimidating. If I had a relationship list back then, he would certainly have been on it. But what would I have had to offer him besides my work?

All our interactions up to that point were rather serious and intense—strictly business. Then I discovered that his son was applying to high schools in New York City, and I mentioned that I went to Regis High School and liked it very much. His eyes lit up. That was the school they were thinking of for their son. "Would you tell us about it?" he asked. "Maybe talk to our son?" He and I soon spoke at length over coffee and he was extremely grateful. We had deepened our relationship for sure.

You may not think much about it, but this kind of thing happens all the time. You offer travel tips to someone. You share what you learned when your child was sick. You refer someone to your favorite restaurant. Usually it seems like pure coincidence or luck when exchanges like this happen. But if you're mindful that you have so much to offer, then the opportunities for you to make such a contribution will greatly increase.

Here are a few facts from my own list that have been the basis of a connection with other people. Thinking of them as contributions has made me more curious about other people's facts. It has led me to ask more questions, and to listen more intently to the answers.

My own facts
1 I was born in New York City and have lived there my entire life.
2 I have five children.
3 I'm half German and half Italian.
4 My wife is Japanese.

5 I've spent a lot of time traveling in Japan and Germany.
6 I became a vegetarian in my forties.
7 My mother had diabetes.
8 I attended Regis High School and Columbia University.
9 I studied computer science.
10 After working in corporations for thirty years, I started my own business.

EXERCISE: So much to offer! (15 minutes)

Now take a piece of paper and make your own list, but try to list *fifty* facts about you. Use the examples above to get you started, then reflect on all the experiences you've had in your life that, framed appropriately, might be helpful to someone else.

Q: I only made it to twelve facts.

That's OK. Just doing the exercise and thinking about what you have to offer is a positive step. When I first attempted this exercise, I struggled because I felt the facts on my list had to be grand accomplishments. Now I know that any part of my experience might be interesting to someone else if I frame it as a contribution. Not everyone will appreciate every gift, of course, but someone will.

Q: I don't mix personal and professional.
Besides, how can this possibly make a difference?

Do you remember the variations of The Trolley Problem from chapter 5, on Relationships? In the experiments, feeling a sense of relatedness to another person made a difference in the life-or-death choices of the participants! The sharing of even a trivial fact you have in common is like a bridge that connects you, one you can build upon with additional contributions.

As for the mixing of personal and professional, that is entirely up to you. You needn't tweet all your facts or post them on your intranet or LinkedIn profile. The point of the exercise is simply to help you realize that you have *so many* things to offer that could be the basis of a meaningful connection with someone else. Maybe you ask more questions, for example, or pick up on cues you hadn't noticed before. Just being more mindful can lead to establishing or deepening more relationships.

Human. Potential.

When we conduct Working Out Loud workshops, we form the audience into groups of five people who don't already know each other. Once they've organized themselves, we ask them to do a version of the fifty facts exercise, and they begin quietly scribbling. Then we ask them to share and compare their lists, looking for facts they have in common or are surprising.

After a nervous pause—*Who will go first?*—the crowd is buzzing. People lean in closer to each other. They smile and laugh. What was a professional business event is now, also, a very human exchange. They see that they have more in common with each other than they might have thought. They see that there's much more to the person sitting across from them than they might have suspected.

At work, many feel compelled to hide behind a mask of professionalism. But people don't want to work with masks, they want to work with other people. Our ability to relate to each other is what can make us perform better and also feel better. That's the reason for the Murakami quote at the beginning of this chapter: "The fact that I'm me and no one else is one of my greatest assets." The stories of Mara and Barbara and the others throughout this book, and all of the contribution exercises, are meant to help you realize three things:

- You have a lot more to offer than you might think.

- Making a wide range of contributions—what makes you *you*—helps you tap into more of your potential by expanding your sense of what you have to offer.

- Your contributions over time are what deepen a sense of relatedness with other people, and that feeling is what unlocks a range of benefits that are better for you, for the people in your network, and for your company.

Something else tends to happen too. As you make more contributions and connections, your confidence increases. You start to wonder, "What else can I do?" Reflecting on your longer-term purpose and possibilities is the subject of the next chapter.

KEY IDEAS IN THIS CHAPTER

- You have a lot more to offer than you might think, including all the many facts about you. They can be the basis of a shared experience and connection with others.

- Feeling a sense of relatedness makes a difference in how people treat each other.

- It's usually not a single contribution that makes a difference, but a range of contributions over time. That produces a cumulative effect, deepening trust and a sense of relatedness with some of the people in your network.

EXERCISES

Something you can do in less than a minute

We all have people in our relationship list with whom we've lost touch. The more time passes, the more we feel bad about it, and the tougher it seems to be to do something about it. You can fix that now.

Pick one person on your list that you've been meaning to reach out to and ask them to lunch. Make it personal: "I think of you often, and I miss our conversations. Would you like to have lunch together?" Look at your calendar first so you can suggest three specific dates as options.

Something you can do in less than 5 minutes
It's such a common practice at this point that most people don't think about it. As a result, well over 90 percent of the people who send me email make this mistake. Though it would only take a few seconds to correct it, they repeat the error over and over every day, missing an opportunity each time.

What is this egregious mistake? *They don't personalize the closing of their emails.*

Maybe you use an automated signature, so the same bland phrase (and lengthy contact information) is appended to each and every email. Or maybe it's just a habit. Whatever the reason, you can do better. The final closing of your message is a signal. If you use an automated or otherwise impersonal closing, it tells the recipient that they are not worth the trouble of a few seconds to sign off with something just for them.

When you avoid the scripted "Kind regards," you offer an additional opportunity for a sense of connection and relatedness. Think of it as a small exercise in empathy. *How would I feel if I received this?* Your closing needn't be long or intimate, and certainly shouldn't be inauthentic. You're just adding a few personal words relevant to the context of the message:

"Thank you again for your kind note. I appreciate it."
"Have a wonderful weekend. Cheers from NYC!"
"I'm looking forward to our call on Thursday. I always enjoy our conversations."

Be different. The world is already full of impersonal communications. When you humanize yours, you will distinguish yourself in a wonderful way.

End your next email with a personal message.

15

Your Greater Purpose

The future cannot be predicted,
but futures can be invented.

DENNIS GABOR, *Inventing the Future*

FOR SOME OF you, this might be the most important chapter in the book. In the Getting Started section at the beginning of Part III, you identified a near-term goal that would help you focus and orient your WOL activity as you develop new habits. Now, before leading you through some more advanced contributions and techniques, I want to offer you a chance to take a step back and think about why you're doing all of this anyway. Having a longer-term view will open your mind to some additional possibilities you may not have dared to consider.

A vision of your future

In *Coach Yourself*, Anthony Grant and Jane Greene describe a method to help you decide what's important to you and what to focus on: you write yourself a letter from the future. It's a deceptively simple exercise. You choose a date some months or years ahead. Then you imagine what has happened during that time if your life has gone well, and how you would feel if you were successful and fulfilled. The variety of the examples in *Coach Yourself* show there's no one right way to write such a letter. What they have in common is authenticity and earnestness, and Grant and Greene offer the following advice on how to capture that in your own letter as you imagine what you will be doing and feeling at some future point.[1]

For it to be real, for it to be useful, you need to engage your emotions. It seems that there is something quite special about writing it down that allows you to reach into your deepest self.

My own letter

I first did a variation of this exercise when I took part in the Relationship Masters Academy led by Keith Ferrazzi. He had us write up our dreams and goals, a short summary of our long-term vision, and three specific results that would tell us if we had accomplished what we hoped.

He also had us describe both how we would feel if we didn't pursue our goals, and how we would feel if we did.

I remember being nervous when I wrote it, and I also remember thinking it was odd to feel nervous about writing something that I never intended to share. Yet once I let go of my anxiety and allowed myself to write, I remember feeling that I could *taste* the future. Here's what I wrote:

My dreams/goals

To live in different countries for months at a time—Japan, France, Spain, Italy (to name the top four).

I would like to write (publicly—beyond my weekly work blog, which was at least a start) and to connect with an audience.

I'd like to create! Books, but also software and other projects. Things that people would use and love.

I'd like to do something genuinely helpful, particularly when it comes to education for kids who may not normally have access to it. (I benefited from going to Regis High School, a free scholarship high school that changed my life.)

Oh, and financial independence... Actually, I don't mind the idea of having to work to earn a living. But the dream is more to be able to research/write/speak/present about ideas and connect with people. Perhaps ideal "jobs" are those of a Malcolm Gladwell, Clay Shirky, or Seth Godin... or Keith Ferrazzi.

Articulating my vision

I will become a champion of ideas. Who will write, speak, and connect. Within ten years. (But taking steps NOW!)

How will I know?

I will have authored a book or other notable content that more than twenty thousand people read. I will have been paid to speak. I can earn a living from writing, speaking, and (only some) consulting.

How will it feel if I don't try, and if I do?

If I don't pursue my mission now, I will continue to live my status quo and... my sense of being special will fade. My frustration at not doing "more" will increase. My (constant) fear of having to earn enough for the next twenty-plus years will remain. My entire life will be colored by the previous two statements.

If I do pursue my vision now, I will be increasingly happy and . . . my sense of peace and inner calm will be much, much greater. My energy and enthusiasm will be much higher—every day. My family will be happy because I'll be "present" and happy.

Four years after I wrote this, I came across the exercise in *Coach Yourself* and remembered that I had done something similar. When I reread what I had written, what surprised me was how much of it was already coming true or still felt right. It seemed as though the act of envisioning the future and writing it down had shaped my thoughts and my actions.

Daring greatly

Writing a Letter from Your Future Self is now an exercise in Week 7 of a WOL Circle, and sometimes people will mention their letter online or share it with me via email. For example, an engineer named Bernadette wrote to tell me that her initial goal was to find a new job in her company but, after a series of small steps, she gradually became more confident and began thinking more broadly. She started considering alternatives that made the most of her talents and aspirations. Soon she let herself dream, and she decided to change course in dramatic fashion.

Bernadette wrote to me about her experience in Week 7, and shared her story. "This just feels so good," she wrote, "It feels 'me.'"[2] Here's her letter.

A letter from my future self: Sometimes you have to take a bigger step towards your goal

Have you ever thought about how it will feel to realize your big dream?

I work at a big company and joined a WOL Circle some months ago. I joined with the goal of finding a new job within the firm. I am an acoustics engineer, composer and musician and landed a job in sound development for exhaust pipes but I realized quite quickly that I am not on the right track.

By joining a Circle one year after joining the company I started working on my network and looking for new opportunities. My network is strong, but there was no new job, and a lot of wishes and dreams inside my heart. And then there was Week 7. The best week ever. I wrote a letter to myself. It was incredibly easy. I was listening to my heart and the text was just growing by itself. Well, I already had that particular dream years ago but I never took the first step because I thought the time wasn't right. But in my situation, ideas started to form and grow: the plan to realize what's inside of me. To break out and do something absolutely DIFFERENT.

Some weeks ago, I finished my Circle and said goodbye to my colleagues at work. I finally took the big step I was first afraid of and I am looking forward to changing my life upside down. Together with my partner, I will set sail soon. As an adventurer and musician, I want to go on a big journey on our 41-foot sailboat with a piano on board composing music.

I want to share my story to show people that it's possible to live dreams, and to help them achieve what they are longing for. I am currently working on my first videos to share on Facebook and YouTube and I wrote my first blog posts. I am not used to being active online and it felt a bit weird at first to write in public but the principles of WOL helped me to feel more confident and to share my story in the process. It's normal that it takes some time to get used to new things in life, but it is amazing to explore and learn about the world, and especially about yourself.

Charting your own course

Sometimes you know the direction you're heading in isn't quite right for you but, unsure of where else to turn, you keep going anyway, saddled with growing discontent and dissatisfaction. Or maybe you just have a sense there could be more that life has to offer. Although your path may well be different from Bernadette's, we can all take steps toward finding more meaning and fulfillment in our lives.

The act of envisioning the future and writing a letter to yourself about it can help you reflect on what's important to you, and open up the potential for changing course. A woman named Isabella, working at Schaeffler in Germany, had that experience and tweeted, "It's crazy that I searched so long for my life goal and then I started with WOL just to find my goal right there in Week 7." Somaya, working at IBM, tweeted, "WOL Week 7! Letter from my future self—didn't even know I already had a long-term goal subconsciously. This exercise delivered that to my conscious mind. Genius move @johnstepper."

It may seem obvious that reflecting on your future can help you shape it, yet I know how uncomfortable this exercise can be. After writing about my future in the Relationship Masters Academy, it took me ten years to do it again.

Ten years later

Every time I updated the Circle Guides I would tell myself, "I should really update my letter." When a few people commented that my example in Week 7 wasn't really a letter at all, I'd tell them, "Yes, I should really update it." I put "write a letter from my future self" on my to-do list, and even started a draft, but years went by, and something inside me resisted writing it. Perhaps I was afraid of what was ahead, or afraid that writing down what success would look like would seem presumptuous, something not yet earned.

Then someone posted online that this letter exercise was hard for them, and that gave me the inspiration I needed. I thought, *If I can't do it, how can I ask others to try?* So, here's my newest Letter from My Future Self.

The instructions say to write this letter for yourself, not to impress someone else. That's what I tried to do. I share it here to offer another public example of what such a letter might look like, and also to serve as a visible reminder of what I aspire to accomplish. To help me write it, I put the timeframe further out than usual. That made it safer for me somehow.

April 24, 2034

Dear John,

Well, here we are: 2034. It's a number I thought I'd only see in science fiction stories. (I still remember when Orwell's *1984* was a distant future.) Now I'm seventy years old. More precisely, we are seventy. Congratulations to both of us for making it this far.

A lot has happened, some of which you hoped for, and some which you didn't dare to dream about at the time. Brace yourself, though. It wasn't easy.

Our family is doing well. The kids are great. As you grew to be more comfortable in your own skin, that made it easier for others to be comfortable with and around you. It took much longer than we both might have hoped, but you made steady progress. The yoga and meditation helped. The move to Japan helped a lot, too. Life is simpler here. You became clearer about what's important and why.

I remember how fragile you were when you started on your own. You were so worried all the time, about making a living, about being a good provider, about your status after having lost your job. If it wasn't for your wife's strength, support, and love, you never would have made it through this period. Be good to her.

The funny part is that things picked up when you stopped trying so hard to make it all work. When you focused on the contributions instead—on making things other people found genuinely helpful and useful—all of the other things you wanted flowed from that.

To be sure, there were blow-ups. Some were near fatal to your business and movement. But then someone would send you a note, saying that you made a difference, and that was enough for you to keep going. The kindness of your WOL community was a source of strength. Never underestimate how important they are.

A key turning point was around 2019 or 2020. Back then, you were like a little boy on a diving board, looking down, uncertain whether to make the leap or climb back down to earth. Some big companies were Working Out Loud, but you were cautious, always unsure or afraid of whether the little success you had would last.

Then you leapt. You started to work with people in factories, hospitals, and schools, looking to help people who need it most. You expanded WOL to include practicing self-compassion and enabling people to make the work they do more purposeful.

In the last fifteen years, you reached a million people. That's a big number. In ways large and small, you've changed how they relate to themselves, to others, and to they work they do. You can let yourself be proud of that.

If I have any advice for you, it's this: Think ten times bigger. A hundred times bigger. Worry less about making mistakes, or about *Who am I to attempt such a thing?* Dare to make a difference. Not for yourself or for your business, but for other people. The world could still use it, maybe now more than ever.

With love and respect,
Your Future Self

EXERCISE: Letter from Your Future Self (30 minutes)

What would your letter look like? Pick a date some months or years ahead (one to three years is a good range) and imagine that your efforts toward your goal have gone the way you hoped. Or use the exercise as an opportunity to consider something more aspirational and longer-term. Then write to your present self and tell the story of what happened.

Your letter might address questions like these:

- What happened along the way?
- What were the keys to making progress?
- How would you have normally approached things?
- How did you do it differently this time?
- How did you overcome setbacks?
- When did you realize you were going to be successful?
- How does your future self feel to be successful and fulfilled?
- How might you have felt in the future if you hadn't made the effort?

Choose whatever format or outline feels right for you. (Some of you may prefer using images of your future instead of writing about it. If so, try a vision board: a collection of photos from magazines or other media that capture what your future self, your future life, will be like.) Whatever format or medium you choose, remember the advice from *Coach Yourself*: "For it to be real, for it to be useful, you need to engage your emotions."

When was the last time you invested thirty minutes into thinking intentionally about your future? Try it now or make an appointment with yourself when you have the time to reflect and write. Pay yourself first, and intentionally shape your future.

KEY IDEAS IN THIS CHAPTER

- Destiny isn't something that awaits you. It's something you create.

- When you visualize your future self and a possible path you'll take to get there, you increase the chances of realizing that future, particularly when you create an emotional connection to it.

- When was the last time you invested thirty minutes into thinking intentionally about your future? Don't wait ten years like I did. Try it now. Sometimes all it takes is setting aside some quiet time for yourself or working on your letter together with a friend.

EXERCISES

Something you can do in less than a minute

Go to your LinkedIn profile and add a short sentence about your goal. For example, after one of the early drafts of this book, I added "Author of *Working Out Loud*." Mara might have added "Kiwi in London, heading back home to New Zealand." Barbara could add "Genealogist" and Mari could add "Composer."

If your goal is to develop a new skill or project at work, write about that. ("Interested in how the Internet of Things can improve what we do.") Or perhaps you're exploring relocation opportunities, or a new topic. ("Would love to work in Brazil someday"; "Want to help young women with STEM careers.") Now when people look at your profile, they'll see more of the real you. That one simple step increases your chances of realizing your goal.

Keep it short. Feel free to try different things until you come up with something you're comfortable with. Then do the same for your Twitter profile.

Something you can do in less than 5 minutes

The inspiration to do this exercise came from Moyra Mackie, the first person I ever called "coach." At the time, I was working in a bank, struggling to write drafts of *Working Out Loud*, and feeling like I was paddling in a leaky canoe—lots of activity but not much progress or direction.

On one of our phone calls, Moyra suggested that I write down what my "perfect month" might look like a year or two out. That timeframe was far enough away to give me the latitude to do different things, yet close enough that I needed to be practical. My perfect month wasn't something like sitting on a beach in Okinawa, but about a way to earn a living while living a balanced life.

So I took a piece of paper, wrote down the days of the month, and started to imagine what I would do each day. I had considered the things I began listing before, yet something about mapping those ideas to specific days in the month made them seem more real—and made me ask myself more questions. Yes, I would like to travel, write, do research, et cetera. But how much? One day a month? Five? Ten? I found myself visualizing my days and weeks. I imagined how it would feel—how *I* would feel. It enabled me to see an example of what a more balanced, creative, fulfilling portfolio might look like. That was a few years ago. I happened to find that piece of paper recently and was struck by how much of it describes my last month, and the month before that.

When you reflect on your own career and life, where are you heading? What's your perfect month?

☑ GETTING STARTED

☑ CONNECTING

☑ **CREATING**

☐ LEADING

16

The Start of Something Big and Wonderful

If we wait until we're ready, we'll be
waiting for the rest of our lives.

**VIOLET BAUDELAIRE, IN DANIEL HANDLER'S
LEMONY SNICKET SERIES**

MORE THAN FORTY years after first hearing the story, its central question lingers in my head: "Felice, what did you learn today?"

"Felice" (fell-EE-chay) is Felice Leonardo "Leo" Buscaglia, a professor at the University of Southern California whose father instilled in him a sense of curiosity and a habit for learning that lasted his entire life. Buscaglia went on to write books about love and give talks that were broadcast on public television in the 1980s. That's where I first heard him tell the story of what he called "the dinner table university" that he experienced as a child, and it has stuck with me ever since.

Buscaglia grew up in a large Italian family that immigrated to America. They were poor but were surrounded by people and love, by food and opera. His father, who was taken from school at an early age to work in a factory, was determined that none of his children would be denied an education. As he writes in his book, *Papa, My Father*:[1]

Papa believed that the greatest sin was to go to bed at night as ignorant as when we awakened. To ensure that none of his children ever fell into the trap of complacency, Papa insisted that we learn at least one new thing each day. And dinner time seemed the perfect forum for sharing what we had learned that day. Naturally, as children, we thought this was crazy.

Not having an answer wasn't an option. So, before dinner, the children would scramble to come up with *something* they could offer. Out of desperation, they might frantically turn to the encyclopedia to find some fact they could use. *"The population of Nepal is..."* young Leo might offer, and Buscaglia describes what would happen next.

Silence. It always amazed me and reinforced my belief that Papa was a little crazy that nothing I ever said was too trivial for him. First, he'd think about what was said as if the salvation of the world depended upon it. "The population of Nepal. Hmmm. Well." He would then look down the table at Mama, who would be ritualistically fixing her favorite fruit in a bit of leftover wine. "Mama, did you know that?" Mama's responses always lightened the otherwise reverential atmosphere. "Nepal?" she'd say. "Not only don't I know the population of Nepal, I don't know where in God's world it is!"

Of course, this only played into Papa's hands. "Felice," he'd say. "Get the atlas so we can show Mama where Nepal is." And the whole family went on a search for Nepal.

Each child's contribution was carefully examined and considered, no matter how small it was. It wasn't so much the specific bit of knowledge that was important, but more the sharing of that knowledge.

Without being aware of it, our family was growing together, sharing experiences and participating in one another's education. And by looking at us, listening to us, respecting our input, affirming our value, giving us a sense of dignity, Papa was unquestionably our most influential teacher.

"How long we live is limited," he said, "but how much we learn is not. What we learn is what we are." Papa's technique has served me well all my life.

What do you share at work?

The daily exchange over the Buscaglia family's dinner table is something that helped them and connected them. Yet sharing learning at work isn't common, despite how valuable and necessary it is.

When I talk to people about sharing work related to their goal, I usually see an internal struggle in their eyes and hear it in their voice. Most of them feel they *should* show more of what they're doing and thinking, but they offer a variety of reasons why they don't. As a result, too many of us wait for something to happen before we decide to shape our future. We wait to be discovered, wait until our work is good enough, or wait for when the time is right. Here are the reasons I come across most often:

I don't know how. The majority of people have never experienced sharing their work online, and some may not have a convenient facility for sharing content at work.

I don't know if it will be useful. For those who know what to do and have a way to do it, there's still an uncertainty as to whether their contributions would be valuable, and they struggle with how to get the attention of relevant people.

I won't get credit. A more insidious barrier is when people feel their contributions won't be recognized. Particularly in a management system of competitive ratings and bonuses, there is a heightened sense of internal competition. Feeling like you're fighting for your share of a finite pie will grossly inhibit your willingness to contribute and collaborate.

I'm too busy. People are increasingly busy, even overwhelmed. So the prospect of taking on any additional task seems daunting. But this is the challenge described in chapter 12, inspired by *The Richest Man in Babylon*. If you don't pay yourself first—by investing in your learning and development, for example—who will?

Papa's method worked because he gave everyone a structure for what to contribute ("What did you learn today?") and how and when to offer it (every day at the dinner table). We'll do something similar in the rest of this chapter. Whether it's uncertainty or fear that holds you back, or it's because you haven't yet developed the habits you need, the exercises here will help make you and your work visible.

Opportunity can't knock if it doesn't know where you live

Remember this one-minute exercise from chapter 7? If you haven't tried it already, now is a good time to do it:

Imagine someone meets you at a meeting or event and then searches for you on the internet to find your contact information or to learn more about you. What would you want them to find?

Wherever you happen to be now, use your phone or favorite internet device to search for yourself. Are the results you're looking at what you would like others to see? How much of your best work is visible?

If you are invisible, you're making it harder for opportunity to find you. Now is the time to take a small step toward improving your results.

EXERCISE: Update your main online profile (15 minutes)

A safe place to start is with your online profile. For many people, that would be their profile on LinkedIn or on the intranet at work.

Almost everyone I know is unhappy with their online profile, yet few of us ever manage to take the time to work on it. This exercise is a chance for you to improve yours. The objective isn't for you to create the perfect profile, but instead for you to take a step toward creating a *better* profile. Any improvement you make now will be a good investment and something you can build on. Good profiles all include three basic things:

- A photo of you smiling and looking at the camera
- A headline (a short description of who you are)
- A summary that fits into a few sentences

Update your main profile now. Whether it's adding one of the elements above or refining what you already have in place, make at least one change. Once you've updated your profile, show it to a friend and ask for their feedback.

Q: What if I don't want to use LinkedIn?

You don't need to maintain any online profiles if you don't want to, but they do have a value. There's a range of reasons why having a profile on LinkedIn, for example, is particularly easy and useful:

- It is seen as a professional site.
- It follows a standard format.
- It is widely used.
- It is fairly static.

In short, creating such a profile is a simple, safe thing to do. It doesn't require much creativity or effort, and it's increasingly expected that you will have some kind of online business profile. (Another safe and easy option is setting up your profile on your corporate intranet or enterprise social network. If you have the chance to set up a profile at work, you should do it, following the same steps.)

It might help to think of your profile as just an online version of your business card, one that is a step toward you taking greater control of your reputation. For example, a WOL Circle member named Teresa worked at a large global company. She added skills to her profile on the company's enterprise social network, and her colleagues used a feature of the platform to endorse her for those skills. Now when it's time for Teresa's annual performance review, it won't just be her opinion or her boss's opinion determining if she's good at a particular skill. That evaluation can be based on public feedback from a variety of people who work with Teresa.

Ten contributions with a single post

Online profiles are just a start. For a next step, here's a simple, powerful technique that will result in a contribution with four benefits:

1 It will clarify your thinking on a topic.
2 It will be useful to others who care about that topic.
3 It will serve as an offer of attention to ten people.
4 It will result in an asset you can use again and again.

The special technique? It's a top ten list. You create a list of ten people or ten pieces of work you truly admire and that are relevant to your goal. For each one, you include a few sentences about why you admire them.

It's an easy contribution to make. Because you're not talking about yourself or your work, you won't trigger any resistance related to possible self-promotion. You're just sharing your opinion of what you genuinely believe is useful. For example, when Mara wanted to connect with businesses building communities in New Zealand, she used this technique to list the top social media influencers there. As you remember, one of the people on that list was a former prime minister who, much to Mara's pleasant surprise, graciously responded. Other people commented on and shared her post, and writing it gave Mara more ideas for contributions to make and people to connect with.

You're not writing to get likes or be popular. You're doing purposeful research related to your goal, refining your taste, practicing ways to make your work visible, and creating gifts for people in your network.

EXERCISE: Your "Top Ten" (15 minutes)

Try it now. Think for a moment about what the theme for your "Top Ten" would be, and write the title here. It could be as easy as the top ten books, articles, presentations, or other learning resources related to your goal.

My "Top Ten" theme:

_____

_____

_____

Next, search your memory and the internet for items to put on your list. Be sure to personalize each entry by adding one or two sentences describing why you found it useful or interesting, or how it might benefit others.

1 _____

2 _____

3 _____

4 _____

5 _____

6 _____

7 _____

8 _____

9 _____

10 _____

Q: I'm stuck. I really don't have
a top ten of anything related to my goal.

I was talking about this exercise to a group of new trainees in our company, and a young woman named Shraddha said she was so new that she didn't have anything to contribute. So I suggested another technique that's even easier: ask other people for their top ten list.

She joined an online group on her company's intranet and posted her question there. Soon, she began receiving responses—on the intranet, via email, in the hallway—from experts around the company. Boom! She compiled the results and created her own top ten, which she posted in the community, leading to more comments and contributions. This new employee who thought she had nothing to offer was now at the center of a conversation with experts around the world, and had created an asset that the entire community could refer to and build on.

Expanding the perimeter of your potential

The more you practice Working Out Loud, the more there is an interplay between curiosity and generosity, between searching and publishing. In the process, you discover more resources related to your goal and also more possible contributions you can make.

Gregory Heyworth, who does research on medieval texts, provides a good example of how this interplay goes well beyond being social or extroverted, and is more about being effective. Heyworth was attempting to decipher traces of the only remaining manuscript of a Middle Ages poem that was badly damaged. He used an ultraviolet lamp to try to detect the writing, but the document was too burned and faded. Other scholars had already given up. In a TED talk, he described what he did when he realized he was stuck:[2]

And so I did what many people do. I went online, and there I learned about how multispectral imaging had been used to recover two lost treatises of the famed Greek mathematician Archimedes from a thirteenth-century palimpsest. A palimpsest is a manuscript which has been erased and overwritten.

And so, out of the blue, I decided to write to the lead imaging scientist on the Archimedes palimpsest project, Professor Roger Easton, with a plan and a plea. And, to my surprise, he actually wrote back.

The simple set of steps Heyworth took—searching for people who could help him, deciding to reach out, crafting a compelling letter that earned a response—sent out ripples that changed his career.

With his help, I was able to win a grant from the US government to build a transportable, multispectral imaging lab. And with this lab, I transformed what was a charred and faded mess into a new medieval classic.

That same lab then went on to "read even the darkest corners of the Dead Sea Scrolls" and make transcriptions from the Codex Vercellensis, a translation of the Christian Gospels from early in the fourth century. Then Heyworth founded the Lazarus Project, a not-for-profit initiative to bring the technology to individual researchers and smaller institutions. That brought him into contact with researchers and precious documents around the world, like the team working on a map from 1491 used by Columbus that was no longer legible. He took all these facets of his experience and became a professor of a new "hybrid discipline" that marries traditional skills of literary scholars with new technologies and techniques.

When Heyworth searched for the work of others related to his goal, and then attempted to connect with some of them, he expanded the perimeter of his potential. By purposefully bringing himself into contact with other people and ideas, he was able to make more progress, unlock access to projects he hadn't known about, and build a movement and a new field of study—all things he could never have imagined when he still considered himself "just a medieval scholar."

The approach Heyworth took—the interplay between curiosity and generosity—is something anyone can practice. It's a habit that Leo Buscaglia's papa was trying to help his children develop, and that you can work on in the next exercise.

EXERCISE: The dinner table university (5 minutes)

Pretend Leo Buscaglia's father is with you now, asking, "What have you learned?" Perhaps it's something related to your goal or recent project, or to an event you attended. It could be something that worked or didn't work. For this exercise, keep it short, perhaps two or three sentences.

Write it down now and post it on LinkedIn, Twitter, or your intranet.

_____

_____

Q: There are so many people who know more about this topic than me. Who cares what I have to say?

Who would benefit from your experiences? *Everyone else like you!* If you chronicle your learning—what you're finding useful, who helped you, mistakes you made that others might avoid, et cetera—then others like you can benefit from your visible work. By sharing your experiences, you'll also give them comfort that they're not alone, along with information that might make things easier for them. Those are wonderful contributions. The experts benefit too, because you're giving them a reason to demonstrate their expertise and an opportunity to be generous in a way that's visible and helpful to others.

The start of something big and wonderful

To close this chapter, I want to share a bittersweet example of someone who had something he wanted to share, but couldn't. David's job was working on technology projects for a group of lawyers, but he also harbored a dream of someday writing children's stories. He had plenty of ideas, inspired by the times he and his young daughter, Lily, walked together and made up characters and adventures. David treasured these moments and wanted to capture them in writing.[3]

Everyone, it seems, dreams of writing that one classic kid's book; the one everybody reads to their children . . .

The first few lines were written on the train (much like I write these now); a world was forming in front of my eyes and soon it would be a best-seller and life would be richer for it. Except, after about half a chapter I stopped . . . then forgot to get out the laptop one night. The next night I had some documents to read for work . . . enthusiasm was replaced by procrastination.

Soon it was pushed to the back; an idea that seemed like a good one at the time, but probably left to somebody else to make good.

After that, David's book project sat on his laptop, untouched. Five years went by.

Like David, we may think our dream is "probably left to somebody else to make good." But it doesn't have to be that way. The start of something big and wonderful is, as it turns out, similar to the start of something small and unremarkable: a simple first effort. As early as 600 BC, Lao Tzu understood that "a journey of a thousand miles begins with a single step." Just contemplating the journey or wishing for it won't get you there. Similarly, all the ideas for making contributions won't mean much if you don't publish that first one.

Five years after shelving his book project, David joined a Working Out Loud Circle. Between what they talked about in their meetings and the encouragement of the group, David took a simple step: he published the beginning of his story as a blog post called "Once Upon a Time," sharing his work for the first time and seeking to get feedback and build connections.

I feel if I chronicle the journey of writing it, share that with you, the audience, then this outlet might inspire me to this time see it through. I hope it's fun getting there, and I hope you can join me along the way.

So, as part of this ritual I'll post some words, perhaps from the book, perhaps from my scribblings I did and now still do for Lily. This week will be the latter, that original poem about our friend the Tin Can Man. I hope you enjoy it.

Once upon a time in a tin can shed,
Lived a tin can man with a tin can head.
A tin can body wearing tin can clothes,
With his tin can feet and his tin can toes.

Will it be a best seller? Maybe not. But it's a step, and that makes other steps possible. The problem for David wasn't related to a lack of talent or curiosity or time. It was that he didn't have the habit of searching, engaging, and contributing. The next two chapters will help you develop those habits.

KEY IDEAS IN THIS CHAPTER

- If you are invisible, you're making it harder for opportunity to find you. A safe place to start is with your online profile, which affords you some control over your online presence.

- When you're not sure what you have to offer, remember the dinner table university: *"Felice, what did you learn today?"* Something as simple as sharing a top ten list of resources that have helped you can provide significant benefits to you and your network.

- The interplay of curiosity and generosity, of searching and publishing, expands the perimeter of your potential. It makes you more effective while it earns you access to more possibilities.

- The start of something big and wonderful begins with a small step. If you're too busy now to pay yourself first, when will that ever change? What are you waiting for?

EXERCISES

Something you can do in less than a minute

Of the three exercises in this chapter—updating your profile, creating a top ten list, and sharing something you learned—which one was the most challenging? Why? If you didn't do the exercises, is it because you don't believe in the benefits of doing them, or you aren't yet in the habit of doing them?

Something you can do in less than 5 minutes

Remember how a simple question from a new employee named Shraddha helped her connect with experts around the world? Like a pebble in a pond, contributions related to your goal can sometimes bring you into contact with helpful people and resources.

Ask a question now in an online community or on LinkedIn or Twitter and see what happens. Be sure to offer appreciation for any responses you receive.

17

Experimenting & Improving

We work to become, not to acquire.

ELBERT HUBBARD

A MEMBER OF a Working Out Loud Circle confided that he had started making his work visible via a blog but, after his posts didn't attract much attention, he grew disheartened and stopped. Since only a few people had read what he wrote and no one commented, he felt like he was wasting his time. "What am I doing wrong?" he asked.

The problem wasn't with his initial contributions, but with his reasons for writing and his expectations for a response. The worst thing he did was to stop, robbing himself of the benefits of sharing original work and the only way he could get better. It turns out he's like the vast majority of bloggers, as highlighted in an article from the *New York Times* titled "Blogs Falling in an Empty Forest":[1]

According to a 2008 survey by Technorati, which runs a search engine for blogs, only 7.4 million out of the 133 million blogs the company tracks had been updated in the past 120 days. That translates to 95 percent of blogs being essentially abandoned, left to lie fallow on the web, where they become public remnants of a dream —or at least an ambition—unfulfilled.

Since that survey, blogging has become easier and significantly more popular. Yet the rate of abandonment remains high. Whether you blog or choose some other medium to make your work visible, this chapter will help you avoid the pitfalls of the 95 percent who don't develop the habit of continuing to experiment and improve.

Think of yourself as a risk-free start-up

In chapter 4, on Purposeful Discovery, I mentioned the lean start-up method that entrepreneurs use, and how the same method can be applied to your career. As a lean start-up, when you have a product or service in mind, your aim is to get feedback on it as quickly and cheaply as you can. Then you use that feedback to adapt, ship a new version, and get more feedback. The mindset of the modern entrepreneur is to try many experiments, knowing that most will fail, and use the learning from those experiments to build something people will value.

This is the mindset my friend should have had when he was creating original contributions, particularly in the beginning. Starting with an audience of zero isn't concerning, it's *liberating*. You're free to explore, experiment, make mistakes, and learn. You have nothing to lose. Better still, with each contribution—each iteration of the start-up of you—you're discovering how to make your work visible and taking another step toward developing the habit of doing so. If you have a mindset that the point of your initial contributions is to get feedback and get better, then you'll be more likely to avoid the fate of most people who give up. If, however, your work is simply intended as a means to popularity or money, you're likely to be disappointed, as that *New York Times* article about blogging revealed.

Judging from conversations with retired bloggers, many of the orphans were cast aside by people who had assumed that once they started blogging, the world would beat a path to their digital door.

"I was always hoping more people would read it, and it would get a lot of comments," Mrs. Nichols said recently by telephone, sounding a little betrayed. "Every once in a while I would see this thing on TV about some mommy blogger making $4,000 a month, and thought, 'I would like that.'"

The Visible Work element is about trying to contribute something, not trying to get something.

A better way to begin

Show Your Work: The Payoffs and How-To's of Working Out Loud, by Jane Bozarth, is an extraordinary collection of ordinary people who are making their work visible. The book includes stories of dentists, landscapers, film editors, teachers, and more. Some of them show finished products, and many more narrate their work in progress. *This is how I did that. This is what I did and why.* One of my favorite examples is the story of Gloria Mercer, a retired schoolteacher.[2] In October 2011, Gloria had surgery on her hand and needed a way to rebuild her strength and dexterity, so she decided to learn how to decorate cookies with elaborate designs. Her first step was to search for information online, where she found YouTube videos, blogs, and Facebook pages that helped her learn the basic techniques. Then she baked and baked (giving her husband the cookies she didn't deem worthy to give to others). She also started interacting with experts online to exchange information.

After a few months, Gloria went beyond searching and started to share what she was doing and learning by posting photos of her latest creations on Facebook, along with comments about recipes and techniques. That inspired her daughter and a friend to learn as well, and soon they were all helping each other improve. Over time, the cookies were looking better and better, and Gloria started giving them to family members as gifts. Shortly thereafter, her daughter established Coastline Cookies, turning their learning into a new business.

Gloria's approach epitomizes the Growth Mindset element described in chapter 8. Focusing on learning and improving rather than a fixed outcome made it easier for her to experiment. Over time, her experiments and the feedback on them made her cookies better and led to other important benefits.

- She learned how to show her work online.
- She received encouragement, which motivated her to do more.
- She discovered other possibilities for applying her craft.
- She enjoyed the process while she kept getting better.
- She developed the habit of posting and interacting with people online.

Show your work

Almost anything related to what you do, how you do it, and why you do it may be useful to others who have a related goal or are interested in the same topic. Here are ten aspects of your work you might contribute that could provide value for people in your network:

1. Share your research.
2. Share your ideas.
3. Share your projects.
4. Share your process or methods for doing what you do.
5. Share your motivations, why you did what you did.
6. Share your challenges.

7 Share something you've learned.
8 Share the work of others you admire.
9 Share your connections.
10 Share content from your network.

For example, Nicola was a member of one of my first WOL Circles, and had recently started a men's image and style consulting business.[3] Its mission is to help you "redefine your look and develop your personal image, giving you the confidence and expertise you need to live an extraordinarily handsome life." Given her focus, here's some original content she might create:

1 *Research:* new trends in men's fashion.
2 *Ideas:* how to dress for certain occasions or wear certain clothes.
3 *Projects:* profiles of men she has styled.
4 *Process:* how she works with a client or how she shops.
5 *Motivations:* why she cares about helping men live handsomely.
6 *Challenges:* her own fashion mistakes or mishaps with clients.
7 *Learning:* new looks she's discovered.
8 *Work of others she admires:* recognizing other stylists.
9 *Connections:* stores, brands, and personal shoppers she relies on.
10 *From the network:* testimonials and other feedback.

This is just a partial list. You could come up with more original contributions, just like the other members of our Circle did each time we met. Throughout our twelve weeks together, Nicola began experimenting with different formats and channels, including blogs, articles in local magazines, and presentations at corporate events. Once she started, she unlocked a stream of other ideas and possibilities. The more she did it, the easier it got.

Here's another example: a third-grade teacher in New York City named Alycia Zimmerman, whom I discovered while searching for educators who Work Out Loud. This list is based on Zimmerman's actual work online, some of it from a public online space she maintains in her name as a resource for her students and their parents.[4] Zimmerman also leverages a powerful network by writing for Scholastic, a leading publisher of children's books,[5] where she contributes yet more original content along with ten other elementary school teachers. Here's a sample of the kinds of things she writes about:

1 *Research:* resources for teachers and parents.
2 *Ideas:* suggestions for teaching time, poetry, and other topics.
3 *Projects:* dozens of examples of work she does in the classroom.
4 *Process:* how she helps kids prep for standard tests.
5 *Motivations:* why she became a teacher and her values.
6 *Challenges:* packing up at the end of the year.
7 *Learning:* new books and techniques she has discovered.
8 *Work of others she admires:* projects from other teachers.

9 *Connections:* people and resources she relies on.
10 *From the network:* third-graders blogging about their class pet.

Zimmerman has written over ninety posts for Scholastic, each one complete with photos of actual work in the classroom. Meanwhile, the work on her own site goes back over five years, evolving as she tries new things. The articles are personal, helpful, and engaging in a way that professional articles rarely are.

The main benefit to Nicola, and to Alycia Zimmerman, isn't popularity. It's learning and connecting. Every time they write about a project or an idea, they think deeply about it and get feedback from others. In addition to that investment in their craft, they're deepening relationships with the people already in their network and, over time, creating a portfolio of contributions they can reuse over and over again, unlocking other possible connections.

When Nicola writes a profile of one of her clients, she can send that profile to each new prospect or to magazine editors who care about men's fashion. When Alycia Zimmerman writes up a project for her class, she can send that to other teachers, administrators, parents, and other people she wants in her network. Each time either of them write, they have more to offer, while making it more likely that other people will discover their work.

Q: I think I get it, but I'm still not comfortable being visible.

That's a common and completely natural feeling, and, as with many skills, you will improve and become more comfortable with practice over time. I remember the anxiety I felt when I wrote my first public blog post, even though I knew almost no one would read it. When it came to speaking in public, just applying to present at a conference made me anxious.

If your anxiety is so great it prevents you from taking a step, take another look at the exercises in the previous chapter and at the lists above. Pick one that feels simple, small, and genuine. At this point, taking a first step and practicing making small, original contributions is more important than any individual offering. The next exercise can also help you.

EXERCISE: What are you afraid of? (5 minutes)

Think about something you'd like to create: a blog, a video, a website. Now list all the fears you have about actually creating it for others to see. Try to list at least ten fears or negative consequences.

Then, next to each fear you listed, write down how likely it is that the fear will actually be realized. Compare those odds with the benefits you'll receive from investing in yourself and developing useful skills like Gloria, Nicola, and Alycia Zimmerman did.

1 _____   _____

2 _____   _____

3 _____   _____

4 _____   _____

5 _____   _____

6 _____   _____

7 _____   _____

8 _____   _____

9 _____   _____

10 _____   _____

It's your choice

Remember that you have complete control over what to share, how to share it, and with whom. All I suggest is that you make a conscious, informed choice. If you choose not to be visible, you have ceded control over your reputation to others. A bad word from the boss or an unhappy client will have more weight than all your private contributions. If you insist on never showing your work, you have given up the chance to be discovered, and have greatly reduced your own odds. Imagine an artist with no portfolio. Or a writer with no articles or books. How would you know what they're capable of?

When you make your work visible, you amplify who you are and what you do, extend your reach, expand your set of possible contributions and how to offer them. The feedback on your work helps you get better faster. If you do this at work, your company benefits too. By making your work visible—what you're doing, why you're doing it, what resources were useful, what you learned—you enable the organization to reduce duplication and accelerate the pace of innovation.

Q: What should I actually do?
Start a blog? Facebook page? YouTube channel?
The answer depends on you, your content, the people you want in your network, and even the tools themselves. All of them keep changing, so it means the answer to your question may change too. A good way to begin is to look at people who are relevant to your goal and see what they're doing. Read blogs, follow Facebook pages, and watch videos related to your purpose. That will help you discover what you think is good, as well as what you don't like. Then emulate the work of people you admire. Over time, as you get better, you'll gradually develop your own style.

Original contributions that anyone can make

The kinds of contributions that Nicola and Alycia Zimmerman make are ones that anyone can make. Do you remember the stories of Sabine and Anja in chapter 1? Both began showing their work as part of their jobs in big companies, using LinkedIn or the intranet. I did the same thing using my company's intranet and followed with a public blog. So did Mara and others whose stories appear throughout the book.

We all followed a similar pattern too. In the beginning, we were extremely tentative. We worried about our first contributions. *Is it good enough? What if people don't like it? What if nobody cares?* We were uncertain if it was even allowed. *Will I get in trouble?* But after the first few posts, we saw that nothing terrible happened, we started to get our first few bits of attention and appreciation, and we started to discover new people and resources. That gave us the spark we needed to keep going.

EXERCISE: Your first topic list (15 minutes)

Something many creative people do is keep a list of ideas handy. This way, whenever inspiration strikes, they can capture the idea and have it available for when they're ready to sit down and create. Now is your chance. Whether it's in a small notebook or on an app on your phone, start a list of topics for things you would like to create. See if you can come up with one thing you might share for each of the items below.

1 Share your research:

2 Share your ideas:

3 Share your projects:

4 Share your process or methods:

5 Share your motivations:

6 Share your challenges:

7 Share something you've learned:

8 Share the work of others you admire:

9 Share your connections:

_____

10 Share content from your network:

_____

Q: My boss doesn't like this kind of thing.
When I worked in a bank and started to write blog posts, a common question from colleagues was, "Are we allowed to do that?" There was a clear sense that "this kind of thing" was frowned upon, either because it violated some policy, or because having the time to write was a sign that we weren't busy enough. So, I read the policies and they were actually quite sensible, ensuring that we didn't, for example, represent the bank in any way or say negative things about clients. We were allowed to share our personal views, and I was careful to do that in a way that was positive and constructive.

My boss was suspicious, though. *Is he doing this to get attention? Should I allow it? Why isn't he using this time for other things?* Aware of this, I wrote on my own time and made sure most of my posts at work were contributions related to my job and our company. Over time, as more people blogged and the benefits of sharing learning were obvious, making work visible became a normal thing to do.

Don't let uncertainty stop you. If your boss or company is uncertain about your efforts to share your work, learn the rules and focus on positive, constructive contributions. As you demonstrate the benefits of Working Out Loud, others will follow your example.

Q: But I don't like writing.

Writing is still the dominant medium on the internet and, like presenting or making videos or any creative endeavor, writing well is a learnable skill. It just takes practice and feedback. Here's a quote that summarizes how important it is:[6]

As soon as you move one step up from the bottom, your effectiveness depends on your ability to reach others through the written or spoken word. And the further away your job is from manual work, the larger the organization of which you are an employee, the more important it will be that you know how to convey your thoughts in writing or speaking. In the very large organization, whether it is the government, the large business corporation, or the army, this ability to express oneself is perhaps the most important of all the skills a man or woman can possess.

That's the management expert Peter Drucker, writing in 1952. More recently, Tom Peters, another management expert, described writing as "a timeless and powerful skill."[7] Even if you don't think you're good at it now, getting better at communicating in any medium is one of the best things you can do for your career. As Fred Wilson, the venture capitalist who developed a habit of blogging every day, noted, "The investment I've made in my communication skills over the past eight years is paying huge dividends for me now."[8] He said he didn't start till he was forty-two, and his story inspired me to begin writing regularly too.

Making bigger and bolder steps possible

When Nicola and I were in a WOL Circle together and she was working on her styling business, she casually mentioned she had written a draft of a novel. "Maybe that will be my goal in a future Circle," she told us. I remember thinking it was a nice idea to write a novel, but I figured the odds of it ever getting published were close to zero.

After our Circle ended, Nicola and I kept in touch. Every so often we would meet, and she would tell me about her latest experiments in her styling business. There were more blog posts and articles, more presentations and ideas for different kinds of services. She also mentioned she was still working on the book, and some days we would sit together quietly and write, each of us absorbed in our laptop with an occasional break for coffee or to check in to see how we were progressing. She told me how she was meeting with a group of writers every week, where they shared their work and gave each other feedback. At one point, she said she had begun reaching out to agents.

Though it happened gradually, the change was obvious to me: Nicola was becoming more confident. She didn't hesitate to try things, show her work, reach out to people, learn, and try again. She told me that the experiments she did in the early days of her styling business made it possible for her to attempt bigger and bolder things with her novel.

Three years after our Circle ended, I attended a launch party for Nicola's first book, *Montauk*. It has been hailed as "a spectacular debut" with "the glamour of Gatsby and the soul of Virginia Woolf."[9] I sat in the audience as an interviewer talked with her about the book, about the wonderful reviews, and about the film rights already being discussed. When she asked Nicola how she became such a good writer, I already knew the answer: she had been experimenting and improving for years.

The day after the event, I met Nicola at a café and we resumed our ritual of sitting together quietly with our laptops. She's already working on her second book.

KEY IDEAS IN THIS CHAPTER

- Almost anything related to what you do, how you do it, and why you do it may be useful to others who have a related goal or are interested in the same topic.

- The vast majority of people making their work visible give up too soon.

- Starting with an audience of zero isn't concerning, it's *liberating*. You're free to explore, experiment, make mistakes, and have fun. With each contribution—each iteration of the start-up of you—you're learning how to make your work visible and taking another step toward developing the habit of doing so.

- Adopting a growth mindset makes it easier to show your work. Focusing on learning and improving, rather than a fixed outcome, is what makes it possible to keep experimenting and improving.

- The regular practice of showing your work helps you tap into a feeling of self-determination. That makes you more effective and more confident, which makes bigger and bolder steps possible.

EXERCISES

Something you can do in less than a minute

Search the internet for "Alycia Zimmerman teacher" and look at a few of the different results at the top. Then search for another teacher you know and compare the results. Imagine both teachers were applying for the same job.

Something you can do in less than 5 minutes

Review the topic list exercise from this chapter, in which you jotted down ideas for sharing research, projects, et cetera. Choose one particular topic, and outline what you might say. Think of it as a very rough draft of a post you might share.

Just a few minutes can help you attune your attention, leading to new ideas for what you might contribute and how. Each time you practice, you reduce any resistance you might have and strengthen your habit of making work visible.

18

When It Doesn't Work Out the Way You Hoped

John, you have something on your trousers.

A FRIEND, RIGHT BEFORE MY BIG PRESENTATION

THE UNIVERSE CAN be a teacher with a perverse sense of humor. Of all the evidence I have to support this, perhaps the most memorable is a presentation I gave in Köln, Germany.

The day started off well enough. I had rehearsed my talk, eaten a fine breakfast, and caught my taxi on time. The first hint of trouble was when the driver asked, "North or South?" Apparently there were multiple entrances, and since we were ensnared in traffic near the venue, I told him I would get out where we were. But the instant I stepped onto the curb I knew I'd made a mistake. There were no signs for the event, no crowds. I walked a hundred yards or so to the door and asked a lone attendant for directions. "Ah, that's the other entrance," she said cheerfully, and told me how to get there. "Just five minutes," she assured me.

I started walking, looking up at the bright blue sky, squinting at the sun. It was getting hot. Then I looked down and noticed a white splat on my shoe. Fresh paint! And it wasn't just on my shoe! I noticed there were white splotches on the bottom of both pant legs and on my thigh. Where did it come from?! I looked around but didn't see paint anywhere. I considered going back to the hotel and changing but I was afraid it would take too long.

Ten minutes later, I was wandering around in a park of some kind, on a path that led me to a dead end at a highway on-ramp, and I was becoming increasingly agitated. After another twenty minutes, I finally found the elusive entrance, and by now sweat had begun to drip down my face and neck. *Perhaps no one will notice the paint,* I thought.

On my way to the restroom, I saw a friendly face, someone I hadn't seen for a year. "John!" he shouted, smiling broadly. He extended his hand, leaned in close to me and whispered, "You have something on your trousers." I smiled a frozen, awkward smile and quickly moved on, cursing to myself and looking heavenward. Once inside the crowded restroom, I mopped up with wet paper towels as best I could, and I headed toward the stage.

Perhaps the most remarkable thing about what happened that day is that, details aside, it wasn't so extraordinary. I have experienced a cornucopia of devious problems with slides, audiences, room configurations, technology—and now paint. In the past, I might have been so upset that I couldn't focus on my talk, but this time I went on and presented Working Out Loud to a friendly, interested crowd of HR managers, and it was one of my best performances. (No one else commented on the paint, by the way, and I didn't ask.)

What's the universe trying to teach me with all of this? I think the point is that setbacks and mistakes and even bad luck are natural parts of the process of experimenting and learning. A growth mindset helps you focus on offering your gift instead of on the outcome. With practice, you come to embrace the universe's lessons with humility and a sense of humor, and seek to find out what you can do to improve next time.

The question that can help you improve at almost anything

Whatever it is you would like to get better at, here's a technique that can help you. Imagine, for example, you're the one about to deliver a presentation. You're nervous and uncomfortable talking in front of groups. But you prepare as best you can, muster up your courage, and deliver the talk. Afterward, you breathe a sigh of relief and ask someone the worst possible question you could ask: *"How did it go?"*

The other person knows you're anxious, and they want to be supportive and encouraging so they respond, "It went well!" In that moment, you miss a chance to get constructive feedback and learn, and the other person is robbed of the chance to help. I realize this exchange is so common that it may seem strange to deviate from it, but I learned a better way from Keith Ferrazzi, who taught me to think differently about feedback and improving. He showed me it's possible to turn a potentially uncomfortable conversation into one that can benefit both individuals and even deepen the relationship.

The problem, Keith pointed out, is the way we frame the question. When you ask, "How did it go?" or "How did I do?" that puts the other person on the spot. They'll be uncertain of what they should say and worried about offending you, so they'll tend to give you a generic, positive response. Instead, Keith suggested, you should explain that you're trying to improve, and then ask, "What's one thing I could do better?" That turns an imposition into an invitation. Now you have given them explicit permission to give you specific feedback. Because of the way you asked the question, it feels like a contribution instead of a criticism.

I've been asking Keith's question ever since, including after "the paint incident" and my presentation in Köln. The question almost always leads to interesting conversations. People seem grateful to be asked their opinion in this way, and they usually come up with something I can do better:

"You should move side to side a bit less."
"That slide was hard to read."
"You should use some different examples."
"You talked really fast."
"You should hold the microphone closer to your mouth."

I listen intently to each bit of feedback. Sometimes I don't agree with their suggestions or may get conflicting opinions, but I almost always learn about some new way I can improve. Each exchange is also a chance to practice offering vulnerability and receiving constructive criticism.

EXERCISE: "What's one thing I could do better?" (5 minutes)

Think of a skill or behavior at work you want to develop—leading a meeting, writing, presenting—and identify the next opportunity you'll have to do it. Now include a note in your calendar just after the time of that opportunity to ask the question, "What's one thing I could do better?"

Q: Who would I ask? It feels awkward.

Empathy is the best guide you have for choosing someone to approach. Imagine how you would feel if you were the person being asked the question, and if it feels like an imposition rather than an invitation, choose someone else. For example, after my talk in Köln, I asked people who came up to discuss it afterward, or who had asked a question during the Q&A. If you're asking the question at work, you might approach someone who has shown an interest in your previous posts, or a colleague whose opinion you trust.

Be mindful that they might be too busy at the moment, or may not be able to provide a useful answer. That's okay. Try again next time. As asking the question becomes a habit, there's a cumulative effective in both your ability to receive feedback and to use that feedback to improve.

Approaching someone for help

Sometimes, of course, you need more than feedback. You need advice, information, an introduction, a reference. Then what? As with your other interactions, the key is empathy and generosity. *How will the recipient receive my request, and is there any way to frame it as a contribution?*

Here's an example from Tim Grahl, who helps authors market their books:[1]

Two authors recently e-mailed me for the first time. The subject line of the first read, "Let's meet." The e-mail shared the author's struggle marketing his book and a request for a phone call so he could "pick my brain" about what he was doing wrong and how to fix it.

The subject line of the second e-mail read, "Interview." The e-mail was a request to interview me for his podcast so that he could share my advice to educate his listeners and promote my business.

Which one do you think got a response from me?

The first email was all about the sender. It had nothing in it for Grahl, and brain-picking isn't an incredibly attractive offer. The second email was still asking for something—the chance to interview and learn from Grahl—but it included the potential to reach new customers for Tim's business, which was something that Grahl might also value.

Before you ask for help, spend time figuring out how the other person can gain something too. It might take some creative thinking on your part, but it will help you stand out and get better results. If you can't come up with a contribution, remember that vulnerability can also be a gift if it's presented in the right way.

The art of asking

Amanda Palmer, a singer and songwriter, spoke about vulnerability as a gift in her TED talk "The Art of Asking," and she later wrote a book with the same title. One of her first jobs was as a living statue. She would stand on a crate dressed as an eight-foot-tall bride and place a hat or can in front of her for donations. Those who gave money were treated with deep eye contact and a flower. Later, as a struggling musician, she often needed places to stay as well as food or equipment. Via Twitter and other channels, she would let fans know where she would be and what she needed. She felt strongly that "you don't make people pay for music. You let them."

Why would anyone help her or pay for her music if they didn't have to? Because they got something in return: the chance to connect with her and be part of her journey. Her vulnerability made that possible. Not everyone helped, of course, but when she asked for money on Kickstarter to launch a new album, twenty-five thousand individuals donated a total of more than $1.2 million. Here's a quote from her book:[2]

Asking for help with shame says: You have the power over me. Asking with condescension says: I have the power over you. But asking for help with gratitude says: We have the power to help each other.

When I needed help with this book—reviewing content, editing, marketing—I thought of the eight-foot bride. I could have pretended to have everything under control, but that would have been inauthentic. Instead, I shared early drafts and offered people the chance to help make it better. I sought out people with specific expertise to see if they might be interested in the book's message and helping to spread it. I acknowledged their contributions with personal thank-you notes and thanked them publicly too, the literary equivalents of Palmer's deep eye contact and a flower.

EXERCISE: Be the eight-foot bride (15 minutes)

Look through your relationship list on page 157 to find someone who can help you, then send them a message. Pick someone who's particularly nonthreatening, and practice framing your request as a contribution, avoiding phrases like "I want," "I need," and "I would like to."

Q: It doesn't feel right to ask for help, especially if I don't know the person well.

Offering vulnerability is one of the most challenging contributions you can make. Being mindful of the following questions can help:

- What would my reaction be if I were that person?
- Why should they care?
- Why am I doing this?
- Is there something else I could have done first?

You may recognize the first three questions from chapter 13, on how to approach people. The first question invokes empathy; the second helps you focus on the value to the recipient instead of the value to you; and the third helps you examine your motives and gives you the chance to rethink them if necessary. The fourth question is specific to asking for help. Before sending an email to someone, could you have offered attention or appreciation? Could you have done some research to see if they've already answered your questions elsewhere?

Is there some other way you could have added value to them before making your request?

For example, as a new entrepreneur, I would surely benefit from the advice of Fred Wilson, the venture capitalist from chapter 6. Imagine I send him the following note:

Hello Fred,

I'm thinking of starting my own company and could use your advice. Would love to buy you coffee and pick your brain.

I have time next week. What days are good for you?

Looking forward to it!
John

With a little empathy, you can anticipate his reaction. Like the first request to Tim Grahl, this email is all about me. I might as well spit on Wilson's sneaker.

A better approach is to put effort into building some kind of trust and sense of relatedness *before* asking for help. I might start, for example, by following him on Twitter and subscribing to his blog. Then I might take it a step further and offer comments. I would be on the lookout for when he posts a question or asks for help, as Mara did when she was searching for people and resources related to New Zealand.

If you think these small steps won't matter, here are some numbers to show you why they can make a difference. Of the ten million people who have visited Fred Wilson's daily blog, only ten thousand (that's 0.1 percent) have commented. A much smaller percentage of readers post a comment regularly, and Wilson refers to these people as "the avc.com community." Now imagine his reaction when he gets an email from someone asking for advice. Would he be more likely to help someone who hasn't bothered to read what he's already contributed, or someone who has offered attention and appreciation and made the effort to be part of his community?

None of this guarantees you'll get the response you want. It just makes it easier for you to reach out and easier for the other person to receive the message the way you intend. Still, you should be prepared for two other outcomes: being ignored and being rejected.

When people ignore you

Tim Grahl offered some excellent advice for people seeking help from others:[3]

When you are in outreach mode, revoke your right to be offended. You're not always going to get the answer you want. People are going to turn you down or just ignore you from time to time. That's a part of the game; that's a part of life. When you don't get a favorable response, take a breath and move forward. Keep looking for ways to help people. Always assume the best of people.

When I sent people a draft of this book and asked for comments, most people didn't respond, and I immediately made up negative stories to explain why. *They don't like the book! They think it was pushy of me to ask!* While this is possible, of course, the more likely explanation is much simpler: they're busy, unsure what to do or say, may never have received my message in the first place, or have some other legitimate reason.

If you don't get a response, try to remember Tim Grahl's advice: assume the best of people and focus on what else you can do to be helpful. That mindset ensures your requests don't feel like burdens, and makes it much more likely people will respond favorably in the future.

When someone doesn't like what you have to offer

There are times, though, when my worst fears *are* true: the person genuinely does not like my work or has some critical feedback. It stings, and sometimes I struggle not to be defensive or upset. When that happens, I take solace in the advice of Seth Godin, who has written about this topic many times.

It's arrogant to assume that you've made something so extraordinary that everyone everywhere should embrace it ... Finding the humility to happily walk away from those that don't get it unlocks our ability to do great work.[4]

"I don't like your work". . . doesn't mean I don't like you. The difference is critical. It's impossible to be a productive professional if you insist on conjoining them.[5]

Dita Von Teese, a burlesque dancer, put it even more succinctly in a tweet:[6]

You can be a delicious, ripe peach, and there will still be people in the world who hate peaches.

So, I try not to take it personally. I make an effort to listen to negative feedback and see if there's something I can learn or change. Then I move on and resist the temptation to dwell on the criticism or blow it out of proportion. If there's something I can improve, then I should do it. If not, then perhaps I'm offering a peach to someone who just doesn't like peaches.

Q: But what if my contributions aren't good enough?

Good enough compared to what? Although your early original contributions may not meet your aspirations, whether they are "good enough" depends on how they're offered and the expectations around them. If I pay two thousand dollars for a vase from a store, I expect a certain level of craftsmanship. If my friend is learning to make pottery and offers me one of his first creations as a gift, I'll cherish it no matter how misshapen it may be.

The more you focus on framing what you're doing as a contribution and offering it without expectations, the easier it will be to experiment and improve.

Continuing to improve without the suffering

My favorite radio personality is Ira Glass, the host of *This American Life*, which I listen to on National Public Radio. After producing more than five hundred episodes of his show, he's won prestigious industry awards such as the Peabody and the Edward R. Murrow Award, and his program attracts more than 1.7 million people every week. But what's interesting about Ira Glass isn't the number of accolades, his loyal following, or his show's longevity. It's that he said, "I took longer to figure out how to do this thing than anyone I've ever met."[7]

There's a gap... what you're making isn't that good... But your taste is still good enough that you can tell that what you're making is a disappointment to you. A lot of people never get past that phase. A lot of people at that point, they quit.

The most important possible thing you could do is to do a lot of work. Do a huge volume of work... It's only by going through a volume of work that you're actually going to catch up and close that gap. And the work you're making will be as good as your ambitions.

Nobody tells people who are beginners. And I really wish somebody told this to me.

If someone is good at what they do, they most likely took the following path:

1 Their early work wasn't particularly good.
2 They produced a lot of work over a period of years.
3 They gradually learned to get better.

Almost universally, our early attempts at almost anything—whether it's a particular skill we need for work or it's telling stories on the radio—aren't as good as we want them to be. The only way we can make it past the gap between our early efforts and what we want our work to become is by doing a lot of work, getting feedback, and focusing on getting better.

For many of us, thinking about all of the work that goes into getting good at anything is enough to prevent us from starting in the first place. But your path to something big and wonderful needn't be filled with anguish. The key is to break down all that effort into small, achievable steps. Focus on one contribution at a time, allowing yourself to feel the joy that comes from doing something that is good for both you and for someone else. Share your contribution, seek to actively get better, and know that everyone creating anything goes through a similar process. Then use the Habit Checklist in the next chapter to help you make more contributions more regularly. The stronger your habit, the less you'll need to think and worry about taking your next step.

KEY IDEAS IN THIS CHAPTER

- It's inevitable that things won't always go the way you hope. The question is whether you get upset each time or learn from what happened.

- People who produce good work often follow a common path: they produce early work that isn't particularly good, work on their craft for years, and gradually learn to get better.

- A good way to improve is to solicit feedback by asking, "What's one thing I could do better?" This helps the other person feel like they're giving you a gift instead of criticism.

- Another way to improve is to ask for help: advice, information, an introduction, a reference. As with your other interactions, the keys are empathy and generosity. *How will the recipient receive your request, and is there a way to frame it as a contribution?*

- You won't always get a positive response. That's to be expected. To help you maintain the right perspective, remember these quotes from Seth Godin, Tim Grahl, and Dita Von Teese:

  - *It's arrogant to assume that you've made something so extraordinary that everyone everywhere should embrace it.*

  - *"I don't like your work"... doesn't mean I don't like you. The difference is critical.*

- *When you don't get a favorable response, take a breath and move forward. Keep looking for ways to help people. Always assume the best of people.*

- *You can be a delicious, ripe peach, and there will still be people in the world who hate peaches.*

EXERCISES

Something you can do in less than a minute

Reflect on something you're good at now. How did you get good at it? What helped you persist, and how might you apply lessons from that experience to your current goals?

Something you can do in less than 5 minutes

Imagine that your child or another young person you know is trying to learn something new, like riding a bike or playing the piano. What would you say to them? Almost certainly, you wouldn't expect them to be excellent when they begin. You would give them encouragement, find reasons to celebrate and recognize their progress, and gently offer ways they can improve.

Now think of how you speak to yourself as you're developing a new habit. Are you as kind and supportive? If not, why not?

19

Making It a Habit

Wouldn't it be great to be gifted? In fact . . .
It turns out that choices lead to habits.
Habits become talents. Talents are labeled gifts.
You're not born this way, you get this way.

SETH GODIN

WHILE I WAS writing *Working Out Loud*, my friends would often ask, "How's the book coming along?" I would tell them it was going well, and they would offer encouragement. These nice exchanges occurred numerous times over several years.

Then one morning my wife asked me the same question, and the conversation took a different turn. She had seen me brooding in front of my laptop during evenings and weekends and was wondering about my progress. When I told her "It's going well," she had a few more questions.

When will it be done?
I don't know. I really don't have enough time.

How much more time do you need?
I don't know.

How much time have you spent on it so far?
I don't know.

How much did you work on it last week? Or yesterday even?
I don't know.

A long, awkward silence ensued. I felt terrible. Inside my head I was wondering, *Am I serious about this book, or am I just kidding myself?*

What I was missing

In *Strangers to Ourselves*, Timothy Wilson writes that while our brains can take in eleven million pieces of information at any given moment, we're only consciously aware of forty. Only forty! It's a dramatic statistic that shows just how precious little attention we have, and why change is so hard. Acquiring a new skill or behavior requires that we focus our attention over a period of time and, since attention is scarce, we have a natural aversion to expending it. As the neurologist Daniel Kahneman writes, "Laziness is built deep into our nature."[1]

The problem wasn't my intention to write a book. It was that I hadn't yet developed the habit of writing, of taking steps in a disciplined, structured way toward accomplishing my goal.

Habits are one way of helping us deal with the complexity of life and all the information in it. The repetition of an act over time decreases the effort required as our brain physically changes. The more we do it, the less we have to think about it, and the activity becomes easier and more automatic. For most people reading this book, even if you've made a conscious decision to Work Out Loud, it's only when you've turned that choice into a habit that your actions will consistently be in line with your intentions. Applying the Habit Checklist will help you take steps, overcome setbacks, and continue to make progress.

The Habit Checklist

Since that awkward conversation with my wife, I have experimented with changing my own habits—from how I work and what I eat to exercise, meditation, and learning piano and Japanese. In some areas, I've made tremendous progress, and in others I'm more of a work in progress.[2]

Based on these experiments and the research I've done on behavior change, I distilled the techniques I found most helpful into a Habit Checklist: eight things you can do to develop or sustain certain behaviors.

Whenever I get stuck developing any new habit or skill, I look at this list and pick an adjustment to make. When I do so, I reinforce a feeling of control and self-efficacy, a sense that I can do anything if I put in the effort. Without exaggeration, applying these simple techniques has changed my life.

THE HABIT CHECKLIST

☑ 1 **Set achievable goals:** It's good to dream big, unless your ambitions are so daunting that you trigger internal resistance, or so vague that you don't know what to do next and never take a step. To make your goals and ambitions actionable, be sure to have near-term goals you can do something about.

☑ 2 **Touch the treadmill:** The progress principle is a powerful thing. Every action, even small ones, make other, larger actions possible. If you're ever stuck, reduce the size of your next step so you can continue advancing. Remember that any progress is good.

☑ 3 **Chart your progress:** By tracking what you're doing, you become more mindful of your efforts throughout the day. Even one visible measure related to your goal, like the time you spent on it or whether or not you made a contribution that day, will greatly improve your chances of making progress.

☑ 4 **Structure your environment:** So much of what we do is based on impulsive, unconscious choices in response to triggers around us. Knowing that, you can purposefully adapt your environment to help you make progress. This can include adjustments to your schedule, your workspaces, your technology, and anything else that makes it easier to do what you want to do and harder to engage in unwanted behaviors.

☑ 5 **Expect setbacks:** All learning and development includes challenges and mistakes. Feeling bad about them triggers resistance. Instead, view each setback as a natural and necessary learning opportunity, and channel your energy into doing better next time.

☑ 6 **Search for the positive:** We're wired to focus on issues and problems, which can be a disincentive, so it's important to periodically reflect on the progress you've made and reward yourself in some way. Positive reinforcement is much more likely to spark intrinsic motivation and lead to sustainable results.

☑ 7 **Find a friend:** Whether it's simply talking through what you're trying to do or actually going through the process together (as you do in a WOL Circle), support from someone else can help you get through challenges and inspire you to keep going.

☑ 8 **Picture the way you'd like life to be:** This is the flip side of the first item on the list. Setting near-term, achievable goals helps you identify next steps to take. But articulating a longer-term vision of the future helps you tap into your sense of purpose. This reminds you of why you're doing what you're doing, and makes your behavior change more sustainable.

Applying the Habit Checklist to your goal

Think for a moment about the goal you identified in chapter 10 and about the relationships you're trying to build. What would your response be if someone asked you, "How's it going?" Would you have an uncomfortable conversation like the one I had with my wife?

Practice using the Habit Checklist now by reviewing each of the items that follow. I'll include an exercise for each item. Choose at least one that will help you make more progress, and do that exercise before moving on to the next chapter.

Q: I don't need this. I'm more of a creative person than a habitual person.

For most of my life, I thought of myself as someone who is better at generating ideas than getting things done. I believed habits and systems were "not me" and would be stifling in some way.

Well, that kind of thinking was unnecessarily limiting, and an example of a fixed versus a growth mindset. The labels I used to describe myself—"undisciplined," "procrastinator"—were not about my DNA or who I am as a person. They were just about my experiences up to that time. As I developed new habits and behaviors, I learned that being creative and being productive are not mutually exclusive, and that the best creative people develop a set of habits that make it possible for them to regularly produce good work. Applying the Habit Checklist helps me do that.

#1. Set achievable goals

"Achievable" in this context means that the goal is both something you genuinely care about and something that has clear next steps in a reasonable timeframe. I list this item first because when you're not making progress toward an objective, it's a good idea to check that you have the right objective in the first place.

A common problem I see in WOL Circles is when people choose a goal that they *think* they should care about, but don't. For example, it's reasonable to want more recognition at work. But if you don't like your job or the people you work with, it's hard to summon the energy you'll need to pay attention and Work Out Loud toward that goal. In that case, it's time to reflect and invest your time in something else.

Other common problems include taking on too much too soon, or choosing a vague goal. Either of these can make it difficult to know what action you might take next. In either case, it's best to break down your goal and set smaller, more readily achievable targets.

EXERCISE: The Goldilocks goal test (5 minutes)

Take a moment now to objectively review your goal, and do so without attachment or judgment. Does what you chose still spark your interest and curiosity? Are you making progress? Check that it's still something you want to pursue, and that's it's not too big or too small.

If your goal doesn't inspire you, consider changing it to one that does. If you're not making steady, regular progress, consider choosing a simpler goal or taking smaller interim steps toward your goal. In developing new habits, regular practice and feedback is more important than objectives you never reach.

#2. Touch the treadmill

In my children's school, for each classroom lesson there is a "Do Now" exercise that's written on the board, a small activity they can do in a few minutes during class. There may be additional reading or homework the students have to do before the next class but, whatever the learning goal is for the day, the teachers recognize the value of students taking a small action right away. If you're finding you're making a lot of lists but little progress, try this exercise.

EXERCISE: "Do Now" (5 minutes)

Think of a small action you can take right now—and do it. Maybe it's a follow-up email to someone on your relationship list, or a quick contribution of attention or appreciation you've been meaning to offer. Pay attention to how you feel after taking an action, and savor that feeling.

#3. Chart your progress

After I had that difficult conversation with my wife about my book progress, I made an adjustment that same morning that enabled me to publish it: I made a chart. It was a simple calendar with a space for every day of the month. In each space, I wrote down how many hours a day I worked on the book. Instead of the story I was telling myself—*I'm writing a book!*—the data on the chart began to show me that I wasn't working on it nearly enough. That was the push I needed to set up a regular writing schedule.

I'm not alone at misjudging my efforts. Self-reports on common activities—such as how much we eat or drink, or how much time we spend on our phones—are notoriously inaccurate. Maintaining a progress chart does two things: it helps you gather objective data about actions you're taking, and it makes you mindful of that data. No actions, no progress. The key is to put your chart in a place where you'll see it multiple times per day. That's what makes you more mindful of the behaviors you're trying to change. My handwritten chart is next to the bathroom mirror, and I update it in the morning and evening. Though it only takes a few seconds, maintaining a chart makes it clear where I need to make adjustments.

EXERCISE: Make your own progress chart (10 minutes)

Your chart can be as simple as a monthly calendar with a space to write down one or two metrics related to your goal. Say, for example, your goal is to "expand my network of people in the HR area." Your chart might include:

- Did you search/read/watch something from your network? (Y/N)
- Did you work on your goal at all? (Y/N)
- What number of contributions did you make?
- How much time did you spend on activities related to your goal?

Decide what you will track on your progress chart and write it down.

Progress Chart Title:

Now, using a blank monthly calendar or blank sheet of paper, create your physical chart and decide where you'll put it. For examples of different charts that I've used, visit workingoutloud.com/resources and click on "Week 8: Make It a Habit." My charts vary quite a bit in terms of what they track and the format, but they all helped me make more progress with less stress.

#4. Structure your environment

In *The Power of Habit*, Charles Duhigg quotes an expert who has developed training specifically for reversing unwanted behaviors:[3]

Once you're aware of how your habit works, once you recognize the cues and rewards, you're halfway to changing it... It seems like it should be more complex. The truth is, the brain can be reprogrammed. You just have to be deliberate about it.

Structuring your environment involves creating or removing such cues or triggers, making it easier for you to follow through on your intentions. Here are three examples.

Schedule the time to do it. When you schedule a specific time that you'll practice an activity—for example, researching people on your list, interacting with them online, drafting contributions that make your work and learning visible—you don't have to juggle your task lists or think about when to fit it in. The less you have to think about it, the less attention you'll have to spend and the easier it will be to do it consistently.

Create rituals. Your physical environment can also serve as a set of cues to put you in the right frame of mind for Working Out Loud. Cues might include sitting in your special writing chair with a special notebook and pen dedicated to your new habit, or sitting with your laptop and a cup of mint tea in your favorite café. Over time, these cues will tell you, "Now is the time to Work Out Loud," and you'll expend less mental energy getting started.

Set up visual aids. These can be simple physical reminders, such as a note taped to your computer. For example, if you asked yourself, "What's the contribution?" every time you sent an email, it would result in dozens of opportunities to practice every day. Over time, you would begin framing things as contributions without even thinking about it. This alone would be a powerful habit.

EXERCISE: Cues and triggers (10 minutes)

Pick one of these adjustments—schedule an activity, create a ritual, set up a visual aid—or create one of your own, and make it now.

#5. Expect setbacks

Understanding that setbacks are a natural part of the learning process was the main subject of the last chapter, and a hallmark of a growth mindset. When you fail, avoid self-criticism and actively look for some learning you can carry forward. Then commit to applying that learning in your next effort.

EXERCISE: Fail fast and forward (5 minutes)

Reflect on a recent failure. It could be an outright mistake, or it could be the failure to do something you intended to do. Replay it in your head and pay attention to the thoughts and feelings you're experiencing. Do these thoughts and feelings serve you well? Do they help you make progress?

Now examine the failure closely and actively look for something you can take away from the experience that will help you do better. Then write down what you've learned and the adjustment you will make next time.

#6. Search for the positive

My parents were raised in an era when "spare the rod, spoil the child" was considered good parenting advice. As a result, perhaps, my attempts at self-motivation are often harsh, overly critical, and unforgiving. They're also not terribly good for producing long-term results. Positive reinforcement is much more effective.

Animal trainers have known this for a long time. It's why they can reliably reproduce extraordinary behaviors in animals while many of us humans resort to yelling, threats, and force. Karen Pryor is a behavioral biologist, pioneering dolphin trainer, and authority on applied operant conditioning—the art and science of changing behavior. In *Don't Shoot the Dog*, she describes the methods she developed and how they apply even beyond animal training:[4]

I began to notice some applications of the system creeping into my daily life. For example, I stopped yelling at my kids, because I was noticing that yelling didn't work. Watching for behavior I liked, and reinforcing it when it occurred, worked a lot better and kept the peace, too.

One of Pryor's fellow dolphin researchers quipped, "Nobody should be allowed to have a baby until they have first been required to train a chicken." When it comes to using positive reinforcement to motivate ourselves to develop new habits, chicken training would indeed be useful experience.

EXERCISE: What made today great? (5 minutes)
One way to help yourself overcome a negativity bias and celebrate positive steps is to keep a gratitude journal. Each morning, the first thing I do when I wake up is reflect on what made yesterday a great day and what three things would make today great, and I write it down

in my journal. It takes only three to five minutes each day, and it's so useful that I never miss a day. This practice has shifted my perspective from one that's overly negative to something more balanced, and that has made me happier.

Treat yourself to a journal that's small enough to carry with you or that you can leave by your bedside table. Every day, actively reflect on your intentions for the day, and reasons for gratitude and celebration. After a week or two, see if you find any patterns for what makes your days great.

#7. Find a friend

Peer support groups have formed around topics as diverse as abstinence, changing eating habits, and public speaking. That's because they're effective, and it's why we form WOL Circles. Going through change together can make it easier and help keep you accountable for acting on your intentions in a way that is positive and constructive.

EXERCISE: Your personal support network (10 minutes)

A WOL Circle is one kind of personal support network, and you can form one at workingoutloud.com. A Circle in India, for example, described the "sharing of experiences, dreams, and aspirations without fear or inhibition." One person said, "I soon realized it was my 'safe space.'" That feeling of psychological safety made it possible for them to share what was difficult to share elsewhere, and know they had been heard. Better still, week by week they took actions that helped them make progress and build their confidence. More than just support, the Circle offered empowerment.

If you're not ready for a Circle, try this simple shared accountability practice with a friend. At the beginning of each week, each of you sends an email sharing what you intend to do and what happened the prior week. There's no judgment or competition, just encouragement and occasional advice. You can complement the emails with a short call (fifteen to thirty minutes) that allows you to talk through your objectives and learning, and offer help where you can.

#8. Picture the way you'd like life to be

Almost any book on change will talk about the value of envisioning the future. It's why chapter 15 was dedicated to the Letter from Your Future Self. Writing the letter is helpful. Even better is to find ways to be mindful of what you wrote.

EXERCISE: What would success look like? (5 minutes)

Review the letter you wrote in chapter 15. Pick an image or other visible reminder of that letter and put it in a place where you will see it regularly. It can be as simple as taping a photo next to your bathroom mirror or putting your letter on your refrigerator door. Think of it as a subliminal reminder of intentions for the future you want to create.

Q: Are some things on the Habit Checklist more important than others?

Each of the items has been useful to me at different times, but the three things I find most useful in attempting to change my habits are charting my progress, touching the treadmill, and structuring my environment. When I initially failed to make headway on this book, for example, it was because I had no data on how much time I was actually investing. When I kept saying I was going to do yoga regularly but failed, it was because I tried to do too much too soon. My defense mechanisms found ways to sabotage my intentions until I found ways to take smaller steps. Changing my eating habits took the longest, largely because I didn't structure my environment. (Pro tip: if you want to eat fewer snacks or drink less wine, don't keep so much in the house.)

The power of habit

Each item on the Habit Checklist will make it easier for you to develop the practice of Working Out Loud (or any behavior). With time, you'll find yourself thinking more and more in terms of contributions and relationships. If you stopped here, that would be enough. You would already have the tools and instincts to earn access to more possibilities.

And yet, there is still more you can accomplish. As you'll see in the next section, Working Out Loud habits can enable you to tap into the collective power of networks, and make more of a difference in your life and the lives of others.

KEY IDEAS IN THIS CHAPTER

- It takes effort to develop new habits, but little effort to sustain them. *Laziness is built deep into our nature.*

- Whenever you're struggling to make progress, consult the Habit Checklist to identify an adjustment you can make.

  1 Set achievable goals.
  2 Touch the treadmill.
  3 Chart your progress.
  4 Structure your environment.
  5 Expect setbacks.
  6 Search for the positive.
  7 Find a friend.
  8 Picture the way you'd like life to be.

EXERCISES

Something you can do in less than a minute

Think of a habit you're glad you have developed. How did you develop it? Which elements of the Habit Checklist made a difference? Were there other things that helped you?

Something you can do in less than 5 minutes

Think of a habit you wish you *could* develop. Which items on the Habit Checklist might help you? Pick one, and make an appointment with yourself for when you can do the related exercise.

☑ GETTING STARTED

☑ CONNECTING

☑ CREATING

☑ **LEADING**

20

Imagine the Possibilities

And you ask "What if I fall?"
Oh but my darling,
What if you fly?

ERIN HANSON

"**I WILL BE** a great leader when..."

How would you finish that sentence? Will you be a great leader when you've mastered the lessons of Abraham Lincoln or Sun Tzu (or Steve Jobs, Jesus, or any of the dozens of iconic figures whose wisdom is distilled in popular books)? Will it be when you're promoted to a higher level in the organization chart? If you're like me, you've been trained to think you can earn the title of "leader" only when someone else gives it to you.

Kevin Kruse, an author of several books on employee engagement, attempts a more precise, useful definition of leadership, beginning with what leadership is not:[1]

Leadership has nothing to do with seniority or one's position in the hierarchy of a company.
Leadership has nothing to do with titles.
Leadership has nothing to do with personal attributes.
Leadership isn't management.

After dissecting definitions from managers and management experts, he offers his own:

Leadership is a process of social influence, which maximizes the efforts of others, towards the achievement of a goal.

I like this definition. It's devoid of the usual tactics and clichés. The phrase "process of social influence" points to how leadership happens over time and how fragile it is. The rest of the definition I interpret as *helps others realize their potential toward some greater purpose.*

Are you a leader?

Up until this point in the book, Working Out Loud has been largely about you and your individual contributions and relationships. Now you will expand your sense of what's possible by thinking about what you and your network might accomplish together.

When I worked at a big company, we used the word "leadership" so often that its meaning became diluted and was usually synonymous with "management" (as in the email we received after every reorganization announcing "the new leadership team"). Since then, I've seen many examples of people who choose to lead by purposeful contribution and connection instead of waiting to be appointed by some authority figure.

When you find ways to connect and include people who have goals similar to yours, those people can feel they are part of something, and that motivates them to go far beyond simply observing or using your contributions. They'll give you feedback that makes you and your work better, they'll share it with their own network, and they'll build on what you're doing. This can turn your work into something bigger and more important than anything you could do by yourself.

The rest of this section includes stories of individuals who began with a goal and a small step and wound up leading movements through contribution, connection, and inclusion instead of by appointment. A memorable metaphor for how this can happen is captured in a short video about a remarkable few minutes at the Sasquatch! Music Festival.[2]

The power of the second dancer

The video is grainy and jumpy, recorded on an older mobile phone. It shows people lying on blankets, listening to music. There in the middle is a lanky guy, wearing a pair of shorts and no shirt, dancing by himself. He looks as ridiculous as I would look if I danced by myself in the middle of a park, which is probably why a stranger started taking a video in the first place.

For a while, the first dancer is alone and oblivious to the crowd. As you watch, you can almost feel the discomfort of others in the park as they keep their distance and occasionally glance over. It's awkward to watch him flail about on his own. After an uncomfortably long time, a second dancer joins him. It still feels strange, but a bit less so.

Shortly thereafter, a third and fourth person join. Now it's a group that's dancing, something that's easier to join. More and more people begin to participate, each doing his or her own dance, and as the group swells things accelerate. The group is quickly turning into a crowd. By the end of the short video, hundreds of people are screaming and dancing, calling to their friends, racing from all directions to become part of the swarm of bodies. You can no longer see the person who started it all. The awkward solo dance has turned into a movement that people want to join.

How the best and biggest movements often start

"Leading a movement" is usually something that emerges rather than something you plan to do, and one of the most inspiring examples I know is the story of a brave little girl named Alex Scott. Before Alex's first birthday, she was diagnosed with neuroblastoma, a rare form of childhood cancer. At four years old, she wanted to raise money for her doctors so they "could help other kids, like they helped me." Alex decided to open up a lemonade stand.

Together with her older brother, she raised two thousand dollars with her first stand, and decided to do it again. Then friends and family opened up lemonade stands, and word spread. As more people offered to set up their own lemonade stands, the network grew and the family shared stories of stand volunteers and other children like Alex who were dealing with childhood cancer. Children in other parts of the US began setting up stands. At this point, they had raised two hundred thousand dollars and set a goal to raise a million, and the entire family was invited to talk about it on the *Today Show*[3] and other national television programs. By the time Alex was eight years old and terminally ill, they were starting to count stands in the hundreds. That led to yet more news coverage and more people participating and contributing. The foundation website describes it as "One simple idea, a world of change."[4]

Alex Scott took the "simple" idea of holding a lemonade stand and combined it with the cause of childhood cancer, unknowingly becoming the catalyst for something much larger than she had imagined.

When Alex set up her first lemonade stand, her network consisted of just her family and their friends. But as the network grew, so did the set of possibilities. Alex's parents went on to publish a children's book called *Alex and the Amazing Lemonade Stand*. A documentary called *Alex Scott: A Stand for Hope* aired across the United States (that alone raised three million dollars). Corporate sponsors joined the movement, and the range of the foundation's activities, as well as their impact, continued to grow. Ten years after the movement began, Alex's family spoke to the *Today Show* again. To mark the anniversary, they anticipated twenty-five hundred lemonade stands would raise over a million dollars—their original goal for the entire movement—in *a single weekend*. On the show, Alex's mother reflected on how far they had come:[5]

I wish Alex was here. She would be graduating from high school next week. But her legacy is something that I think I can't even put my head around. The fact that she has inspired so many people to raise money for pediatric cancer research, but also to do something positive in their life, is really something that's to be celebrated.

Today, almost twenty years after Alex had the idea to open a lemonade stand, her foundation is a leading funder of pediatric cancer research, having raised more than $150 million, and it's rated as one of the ten best medical research organizations in the United States.[6] In the beginning, Alex and her family never imagined such outcomes, and their story shows how even the most successful movements often don't start with the end in mind. They just start.

Q: These are nice stories.
But what do they have to do with work?

I picked two extreme examples of leadership—"a process of social influence, which maximizes the efforts of others, towards the achievement of a goal"—so you get a sense for the extraordinary range of possibilities. What follows are some practical examples of people leading through contributions and connections in their workplace.

A simple first step at work

After Mara decided she wanted to move back to New Zealand, she started to meet more expatriates from New Zealand in her company. So she started the Kiwis group at work, an online community where expatriates and current residents could connect to the idea of being from New Zealand. It was an experiment. She wasn't sure if the idea would attract enough of the right people, but it took only a few minutes to create the online site. She enjoyed contributing there, meeting new people, and learning what made each of them care about New Zealand. If the idea attracted enough people, Mara could wind up being the linchpin Kiwi at her firm, opening up new job possibilities. Or she might go even further and help other companies create their own version of Kiwis, perhaps even connecting all of them to the Kiwi Expat Association, which connects "Kiwis and New Zealand business to over 500,000 Kiwis globally."[7]

Meritxell (pronounced meh-ree-tsell) worked in Barcelona, one of the smaller offices in her company, and she cared about empowering women in the workplace. So Meritxell decided to contribute to a newly created group called enRed—"network" in Spanish. She started organizing events in her office and discovered that women were interested. The audiences kept growing, enRed became the firm's most popular group in the Spanish office, and Meritxell became a leading contributor. That experience encouraged her to reach out to women's groups in other locations in the company so she could connect them too. Her small first step helped her build a global network of colleagues and gave her new ideas for other kinds of movements she might want to create.

Barbara, the genealogy and corporate history enthusiast from chapter 10, took a similar approach. She started by creating an online community to connect all of the people who cared about her company's history. She didn't know how many people would be interested, so she started off small. She might just connect a few other history buffs. Or she could discover that many people cared and were waiting for someone to lead them.

This pattern can apply to almost any idea. Sabine from chapter 1 also did something quite similar at work, using the intranet to connect with people who cared about new methods in Human Resources. Anja used her company's collaboration platform to connect with other secretaries who wanted to modernize their skills. You can do it too, using the tools at your company to find people who care about the topic or goal you've chosen.

You start with small contributions and experiments and learn from them. Then you keep contributing, trying new things, refining your ideas, and building more relationships, as we've been describing throughout the book.

Q: What if I don't work in a large organization?

If you don't work in a big company, look for other kinds of organizations for people like you and leverage those, just as Jordi Muñoz did in chapter 1 with the drones community. Go to where people like you are already congregating, either in person or online, and think of that as your organization. Then look for ways to contribute and connect there.

EXERCISE: What's your lemonade stand? (10 minutes)

Take a few minutes to think of an issue you care about. It can be related to your current goal or to a difference you want to make in the world. Don't worry about whether it's a grand ambition or a small positive change. Movements come in all shapes and sizes, and they all need people to lead through contributions. Write down what you choose.

If I were to lead a movement, our goal would be:

_____

_____

Now what would be the equivalent of a lemonade stand for you and your network? Perhaps you create an online group on your intranet related to the mandate you just wrote down, or organize a "lunch-and-learn" in your company where an internal expert gives a talk, or write a blog post on your "Top Ten" related to your purpose. There's no need for a big event or anything that costs much money. Just try a small experiment—a simple way to make your idea visible and connect people to that idea and to each other.

Write down some ideas now.

_____

_____

_____

_____

_____

Q: Why do I need to lead a movement anyway?
The point isn't that you *need* to lead a group, but that you could if you wanted to. If you care about something, it's likely there are others who care about it too, and you

can use your Working Out Loud skills to connect those people, lead via your contributions, and accomplish something together that you couldn't do alone.

Daniella's movement

I met Daniella at a Working Out Loud event, and learned how she is turning a topic she cares about into a movement that connects and includes others to make a difference she could never have made on her own. When she started, she had the same doubts and fears we all have. But by taking small steps over time, with feedback and peer support along the way, she is making something wonderful emerge. Her story, which she shared on LinkedIn, is a good example of leadership.[8]

I was born in Brazil. I live already 17 years now in Germany. I am a woman. I am an engineer. I am a mother of a 9-year-old girl.

When I first arrived in Germany people used to ask me, "What do you do for a living?" They tried to guess and always came up with something like: English or German teacher, Social Assistant, or something other related to teaching, languages or social services . . .

When I replied: I am an Electrical Engineer, they always replied: "Oh, I wouldn't have guessed. It is very unnatural for a woman, don't you think?" I hate this stereotype. I wondered: "Why is that?"

Then I participated in my first WOL Circle. As I went on my journey of Purposeful Discovery, the idea of finding ways to awaken the interest of children for science and technology at an early age wouldn't leave me alone.
But what could I do about it?

What could her lemonade stand be? Her first small step was to join a local association in her hometown in Germany called "Women in Engineering." There she met like-minded people and learned about a wide range of experiments, including one that brings skilled engineers into schools to conduct physics experiments with small groups of children, exposing both girls and boys to engineers and technical careers and giving them the chance to "explore their skills of implementing, experimenting, observing, and presenting."

Daniella used the twelve weeks of her WOL Circle to build relationships with people who could contribute in some way. She needed engineers to volunteer to visit schools during work hours, schools that would allow them to visit, teachers that would give them access to their classrooms, and funders for the resources needed to do the experiments. It was daunting, but Daniella said she "was getting better and better in my purposeful networking." Within a few months she was ready for the first experiment.

We were greeted at the school by very curious and excited children. We experimented with fourth grade children on the subjects of Magnetism, Acoustics and Equilibrium, where the children worked on creating a magnetic race track, a rotating disk siren, and a tumbler toy. We were 5 engineers from 5 different companies present as physics-coaches: myself as electrical engineer working on automotive mobility, a civil engineer designing bridges, a mechanical engineer designing a rocket turbine, another one that designs prosthetic legs and a transport engineer that designs train-beds.

Local newspapers ran articles about what she was doing and that helped her reach more people. Daniella went on to do more experiments, find more volunteers, and visit more schools. What she's doing is full of challenges and uncertainty, and yet she describes a wide range of benefits from her experience so far.

I rediscovered my passion for inspiring children. Since participating in my first WOL Circle I feel connected, I feel that I finally learned what networking is all about and I was able to find similar thinking individuals to start a movement. I feel motivated to contribute leading with generosity for creating a better and inspiring world to our future generations.

Daniella started with a cause she cared about, looked for others who also cared about it, and found ways for them all to contribute and connect. *That is leadership.* Imagine how empowered you would feel if you could bring ideas to life like that. Think of what your organization would be like if more people approached issues and opportunities like Daniella—with generosity, creativity, and persistence. That is what you can do with your Working Out Loud skills.

Nine ways to lead by contribution

Once I recognized the power of connection and inclusion, I started noticing how people I admired interacted with members of the movements they led. The venture capitalist Fred Wilson, for example, speaks directly to his audience, often asking questions or challenging them to debate a particular topic. Then the comments take on a life of their own, going well beyond Wilson's original post, as members of the network keep adding to the discussion. In Humans of New York, Brandon Stanton highlights stories of others, and provides a safe place for readers to interact with each other, as evidenced by these comments:

"I think the best part of the blog is the comments made by people. Their reaction to the posts is just as important in the experience of this blog as the post itself."

"Brandon, do you ever have to pinch yourself to make sure you aren't sleeping? Look at what has become of what you started. An amazing community, brought together by such simple things... pictures and words. Finding a new post by you is like a little present."

Here's a list of nine different ways you can contribute to your movement by engaging the people in it:

1 **Respond.** If someone takes the time to comment on your work or ask a question, respond in a timely, personal way.

2 **Let them comment on your work in progress.** Share your unfinished work so people can shape it and feel they're a part of the process.

3 **Let them build on your work.** Encourage others to extend what you're doing, rather than trying to control or protect it.

4 **Share their reactions to your work.** Highlight some of the things people say or do in response to your work.

5 **Talk to the audience.** The more naturally and directly you speak to your network, the more they will be able to relate to you and care about what you're doing.

6 **Let the audience talk to each other.** Make a point of connecting people in your network and encourage them to respond to the comments of others.

7 **Show their work.** Showcasing examples of how others are applying your ideas is a way to recognize people in your network while providing social proof that the ideas are spreading.

8 **Invite them to be part of something.** Letting your network know when you're traveling or attending an

IMAGINE THE POSSIBILITIES **333**

event, and that you are open to meeting them in person, is a wonderful way to deepen the relationship.

9 **Share their stories.** Profile people who have been particularly affected by your work.

One way to ensure your movement is not all about you is to make it about others. Enabling and encouraging an audience to be a part of your work helps to amplify it. There's no one set of instructions or style for engaging your network. It can and should be a personal, authentic way to relate to people who care about what you care about.

EXERCISE: Who are the best leaders you know? (5 minutes)

What movements inspire you? Think of groups or communities you belong to, the people who lead them through their contributions, and how they engage others. What attracts you to the group? What happens there? Is it all about the leader, or do others participate and interact? Try to write down at least three movements you like, and why you like them.

EXERCISE: Leading by connecting and including (5 minutes)

Leadership includes making it easy for others to follow you, and to make their own contributions. Think of someone who has shown appreciation for your work and thank them for it with a personalized tweet, email, or LinkedIn message. It could be a few short sentences like this:

Thank you for your comments and for being so supportive. I appreciate it. You inspire me to keep improving.

The WOL movement

For most of my life, I thought of a movement as something you join, like the civil rights movement or the women's movement. Movements were organized and important. Larger-than-life people started them, not people like me. Then I listened to a TED talk by Seth Godin on "tribes,"[9] in which he describes how it's easier than ever to find or form movements, whether it's a group of people who make balloon animals or who band together to make a difference; whether it's ten people or ten million. After all, a movement is simply the process of moving people from one position to another. At the core of any movement is an idea, a quest for change that draws people to it and makes them want to contribute and become part of something. The leader, the person Seth Godin calls the "linchpin," is the person who brings it all together through their contributions and connections.

For Working Out Loud, my first lemonade stands were all small experiments. I tried different ways to connect people: blog posts, presentations, webinars, and lunchtime sessions in the cafeteria. Each small success and failure taught me something new. I gradually learned how to engage others using the nine contributions I just listed, and that led to more opportunities for including others and having them shape my work.

Richard Martin
@IndaloGenesis

2nd time I have read a draft of @johnstepper's Working Out Loud. It will be a widely admired, greatly appreciated book. Kudos #wolweek #wol

11:16 AM · 12 Jun 14 · Twitter for iPhone

3 Retweets **5** Likes

In writing this book, for example, I struggled on my own for well over a year with little to show for it. Then I shared a draft with two close friends. Their responses? "Thank you for trusting me with this," and "It means a lot to me that you trust my opinion." I was asking them to spend time reading my unfinished work and *they were thanking me!* Their early feedback and encouragement motivated me to keep writing and to make the book better. Over the next year, I wound up sharing more drafts with over a hundred people, most of whom I had never met in person and many of whom were complete strangers. Some of those people, now more invested in the project, helped spread the word about the book because they rightly felt they were a part of it.

As the WOL movement grows, so does the range of contributions from the people in it. They form WOL meet-ups and create WOL artwork. They translate existing materials and test new ones. They form online WOL groups inside their companies and launch events and campaigns to spread it. They share Circle selfies in Week 12 and their personal stories, including challenges, successes, progress, and aspirations. They help each other.

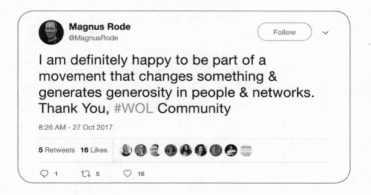

Magnus Rode
@MagnusRode

Follow

I am definitely happy to be part of a movement that changes something & generates generosity in people & networks. Thank You, #WOL Community

8:26 AM - 27 Oct 2017

5 Retweets 16 Likes

1   5   16

Harald Schirmer
@haraldschirmer

Follow

can you feel it? ##WOL is becoming a movement right now - #sharing #networking #purpose Let's activate the critical masses + second dancers

1:10 AM - 21 Oct 2017

22 Retweets 63 Likes

2   22   63

A twenty-five-year-old leader

The story of Anne-Marie, a friend and a member of one of my first WOL Circles, shows how far you can take the ideas in this chapter. Though she's half my age, she has shown me how to lead through "a process of social influence, which maximizes the efforts of others, toward the achievement of a goal."

Anne-Marie and I worked on the same team at the same big corporation for several years. She's smart, but she's not privileged in terms of wealth or family connections. When I first met her, she had an entry-level job and was living in London with her four siblings and her parents, who had emigrated from Nigeria. She was hoping to earn enough to buy a small place of her own.

Her lemonade stand was a blog post.

Anne-Marie's job involved helping people in our large, global company collaborate using an enterprise social network. She thought others might be interested in this work, so she applied to speak at a conference, the Grace Hopper Celebration of Women in Computing, and was invited to be on a panel. When our company wouldn't pay for her travel expenses, she scraped up enough money for a cheap ticket and went anyway. At the event, she heard a talk on how the number of women in technology had been in free fall for the previous thirty years. As someone who had studied math and computer science, she felt she had to try to change things somehow.

Her first step was to write about what she learned at the conference. She had started a blog about ten months earlier, writing on topics as diverse as the Olympics and advice to incoming university students. But after the conference, she started to focus her writing on a particular theme:[10]

Women in technology have a duty to use our technical powers for good. To develop apps, to help deal with major societal problems and issues, and to educate future generations so they're empowered to do so too.

Then Anne-Marie started using Twitter to find people already working to support women in technology. Two months later, she was clear on her purpose:[11]

I want to help girls realize their destiny in Science, Technology, Engineering, and Mathematics (STEM) Careers.

She created a new organization called the Stemettes, bought the stemettes.org domain name, and started blogging about it right away. The purpose of the Stemettes would be to create "a series of events to inspire, connect, and motivate the next generation of females into long-lasting, happy STEM careers."

Anne-Marie told me, "If you don't tell anyone about your idea, then no one else can tell others about your idea." Although she was still at the earliest stage of planning, she published her thinking in the hopes that others could build on it. From the very first posts, she asked for help and included others to be part of the mission:

We need a core team of impassioned individuals who can offer guidance, advice, their thoughts, and some time for honing these ideas. People who have run events before are very welcome!

The initial scope is the UK, but in "working out loud" I hope that others will be able to participate—and I also hope to leverage formats, resources, and lessons learned from around the world.

Then Anne-Marie took what she wrote and started using every channel she could to tell people about Stemettes: "Hey, I wrote a blog about this with three things I want to try." People responded with encouragement and offers of help via the blog, Twitter, and email. That's how she found her first speakers for an event, and students and organizations who were interested in attending.

She approached companies, asking if they could offer free meeting space and a few hundred dollars of support, enough money to serve pancakes and buy some supplies.

In one sense, nothing dramatic happened at her first event. No huge crowd; no big news. But it was a step, an experiment that helped her learn and that made other steps possible. The positive feedback during and after the event gave Anne-Marie confidence that there was a need for what she was doing, and she channeled that confidence into bigger experiments. With each step she was getting better at finding funding sources and spreading the word. More people came to the second event, and an executive at our firm approved funding for the third event after reading about Stemettes on our company's enterprise social network.

Anne-Marie kept trying new things almost every month. Not everything went well—an event might attract fewer people than she had hoped or there would be some technical glitches—but she learned from each mistake and got better. Within six months of her first blog, Stemettes was attracting more partners, more girls interested in technology, and more funding. Now they were raising thousands of dollars, and Anne-Marie was gradually creating a network of partnerships whose support—financial, logistical, and technical—allowed Stemettes to do bigger, more significant things, such as running weekend-long hackathons and workshops to teach girls to code. They were also attracting more attention.

A hackathon with eighty girls led to a two-page feature in the *Sunday Observer*. Then the *Evening Standard* wrote about Stemettes and featured Anne-Marie as one of the "Top 1,000 Londoners." Next was the *Times of London*. She was working at her desk when she got a call from the British television network ITV, who wanted her to appear that evening. "We saw you in the *Times*," they said. Anne-Marie wasn't even aware she was in the paper and rushed out to buy a copy.

Anne-Marie and Stemettes were now caught up in a virtuous cycle. Connections and networks unlocked access to yet more connections and networks. An opportunity for Anne-Marie to speak at an event sponsored by the European Union led to a request for her to deliver a presentation in Brussels, and then an article in the *Guardian* titled "How Can We Have More Female Entrepreneurs?"

She was invited to 10 Downing Street to meet the prime minister, and then to Buckingham Palace, where she was surrounded by 350 of the top people in technology in the UK. (I remember our team's reaction when Anne-Marie shared a photo of her shaking hands with the Queen. We looked at each other with a combination of shock, amazement, and pride that "one of us" could accomplish such extraordinary things.) Shortly afterward, Anne-Marie got invited to a London Tech Week event, where she sat at a table with Mike Bloomberg (CEO and owner of Bloomberg L.P., and former mayor of New York), Tim Berners-Lee (inventor of the World

Wide Web), and Jimmy Wales (founder of Wikipedia). She told me it was "a pinch-yourself moment." These events created more opportunities for funding and new possibilities for helping more young women, including a tech incubator that lasted an entire summer and helped girls create their own companies.

"What will she do next?" we all wondered. Anne-Marie had developed so many new skills and connections that she had created a wide array of wonderful possibilities. She eventually decided to work on Stemettes full time, and at the latest count they have helped more than forty thousand young girls across Europe. Success hasn't been a neat line of carefully planned steps along a well-traveled path. It has instead been Purposeful Discovery, each step producing learning and connections, and increasing the set of possibilities. Her story brings to life all the ideas in this book:

- By making her thinking and work visible, Anne-Marie discovers people and her purpose.

- By framing what she does as a contribution toward that higher purpose, she does work that helps others and is also good for her personally.

- By experimenting and learning from her mistakes, she continues to get better.

- By regularly doing work that's visible, she creates a growing set of evidence of her commitment and inspires others to join her growing network.

- By leveraging and linking other networks, she's able to scale her contributions and make an even more positive impact that continues to lead to new possibilities.

What can *you* do?

When you view your work as a strictly solo activity, when you're the only dancer, it can be both uncomfortable and lonely. Looking for and enabling others to join you can fundamentally change your work and how you feel about it. While few people may go on to lead movements, all of the ideas and exercises up to this point in the book— practicing the five elements of Working Out Loud—have prepared you for doing so. You've practiced empathy and a range of ways to deepen relationships. You've practiced making your work visible and how to frame it as a contribution. You've practiced ways to engage and include people.

You're ready. Of course, you don't *need* to discover a personal mission and build a network that transcends your individual concerns. You don't *need* to make a positive impact beyond what most people would imagine is possible. But you can if you want to. You have a choice.

In the next chapter, you'll meet people who are choosing to lead a particularly challenging kind of movement: changing the culture of their company.

KEY IDEAS IN THIS CHAPTER

- Leadership isn't a title granted to you, it's something you earn over time based on your contributions to others. It is, as Kevin Kruse writes, "a process of social influence, which maximizes the efforts of others, towards the achievement of a goal."

- Although Working Out Loud has to this point been largely about you and your individual contributions and relationships, your goal can be what you and your network can accomplish together.

- Many movements start with a small first step—as simple as setting up a lemonade stand—that makes other steps possible, gradually attracting and engaging a network of people who care about the movement's core idea.

- Your lemonade stand at work can be as simple as a blog post like Anne-Marie's, or a lunch-and-learn, or any small step that makes your idea visible and encourages other to contribute too.

- Anne-Marie's path to building and leading a movement that helped forty thousand young women is a good example of Purposeful Discovery. Each small step led to new learning and connections, and increased the set of possibilities. Her story includes all of the five elements of WOL and illustrates how putting them into practice can lead to opportunities for accomplishment as well as fulfillment.

- Building a movement is rare, but developing the skills and habits of Working Out Loud have prepared you for creating one if you want to.

EXERCISES

Something you can do in less than a minute
Search LinkedIn and Twitter for the hashtags #wol and #workingoutloud. What do you find? What are people saying? Is there one voice or many? Are they all talking about themselves, or is there interaction between people?

Something you can do in less than 5 minutes
Think of your own lemonade stand and the movement you might like to create. Imagine if, like Anne-Marie, your first small steps led to something big and wonderful.

What might it look like? How would it feel? Allow yourself the luxury of imagining how you might contribute and connect and make a difference. Try to suspend all fear and doubt. Set a timer, and make sure you use the full five minutes.

21

Changing the Culture of Your Company

For individuals' behavior to change, you've got to influence not only their environment but their hearts and minds.

CHIP AND DAN HEATH, *Switch: How to Change Things When Change Is Hard*

I WAS SITTING at a luncheon on the forty-seventh floor, surrounded by a beautiful view of downtown Manhattan, listening to our regional deputy CEO talk about our organization's new culture program. Part of the program was a set of corporate values that had recently been announced with some fanfare. After the talk, a senior business executive at our table had a suggestion for how to change the culture at our company.

"I'll tell you what they should do," he said. "They should put posters with the values everywhere. Then everyone would remember them." As if to underscore how simple it would be, he continued, "I bet you could do it for less than a million bucks."

Although he was a smart, successful man who managed a complex business, he had no clue about what it takes to change people's behavior. He also wasn't alone. Senior management forced us go to mandatory meetings to hear about the new values and instructed us to "cascade the message" to our teams. We were told to "live the values" without being told how they would translate into our everyday work.

In one division, change management consultants were hired to help everyone understand how things would work as part of a transformation program. After many months and several million dollars, we wound up having thousands of people play a board game so we could act out, over an hour, how the transformation might affect us and our work.

You would think it's obvious that people don't change just because they attend a mandatory meeting, play a board game, or memorize a list of words that inevitably include "teamwork" and "innovation." But these activities are easier to implement and measure than actually changing behavior, so that's what many organizations choose to do.

I share these stories not to be cynical but to show how even bright managers with plenty of resources can get things wrong when it comes to organizational change. Although they're well aware of the tremendous waste of individual and institutional potential their organization may face, they're flummoxed when it comes to how to make a difference in the culture of the company.

Like most people, I figured there wasn't much I could do about it. Sure, my colleagues and I would complain about "the way things are around here." We would talk about the need for change in the company's management or strategy or policies (or all three). But what could any one individual do? Thinking we were powerless, we passively watched, year after year, as cultural transformation programs came and went. And we waited, and waited, and waited for change.

What else could you do?

A different approach to changing the culture

My exposure to a different approach began with a video call from my office. A colleague in Frankfurt had arranged a meeting for a dozen or so people in Germany who had read about WOL and were interested in learning more. One of the attendees was Katharina Krentz at Bosch, a company with more than four hundred thousand employees around the world.

Part of Katharina's job at the time was to build online communities where employees could share knowledge and collaborate, and it was challenging. She felt Bosch had the technology it needed, and had a well-communicated strategy to be "an agile, highly connected company," but something was still missing: behavior change. The habits of most employees were just too deeply rutted.

When Katharina read about Working Out Loud, she felt it might help with the missing piece. The five elements described the kind of mindset she was hoping to spread, and Circles were a method for helping people develop the skills and habits they would need to put that mindset into everyday practice. So, Katharina went to her manager and suggested forming a WOL Circle at work, and she received an unambiguous response: "No." Her boss felt they were already too busy, and it wasn't the right time to try something new.

Undeterred, Katharina started a Circle on her own time with a few other colleagues. She liked it, told some friends, and a few more Circles formed. Then she wrote about her experience on her company's collaboration platform and formed an online WOL community there to spread the word. Soon there were a dozen or so Circles, and she had enough positive feedback that her manager encouraged her to keep going.

Like the leaders in the previous chapter, Katharina kept experimenting and learning and, as the movement grew, looked for ways to connect and include others who wanted to contribute. She organized volunteers into a WOL Team, and as a group they translated the Circle Guides into German, created WOL events in different divisions and locations across the company, and supported Circles as they spread. As a result of how the team worked together in this self-organized, self-managing way, they were recognized by the German social network XING with the New Work Award for teams.[1]

When a Circle ends at Bosch, the WOL Team encourages them to share their "WOL moment" and fill out a detailed survey. By the time the online WOL Community grew to a thousand people, the testimonials and positive survey results made it possible to get Working Out Loud listed in the company's official learning catalog and to introduce Circles to new employees as part of the corporate onboarding process. With this kind of momentum, Katharina decided to approach the board member responsible for HR and ask him to sponsor WOL in the company. Not only did he say yes, he also agreed to issue a press release about it:[2]

As working in networks and using digital opportunities are key skills for all of us in the digital age, Working Out Loud (WOL) is something that is important to me. And these skills are also very important for Bosch. WOL Circles are a hands-on method to acquire these skills. I am impressed by the speed with which the topic has spread within Bosch and by how positive the worldwide feedback is. I am told again and again that the method enthuses and surprises associates with completely different backgrounds because it is so versatile and yet simple. And finally I have been asked to take over the sponsorship in such a charming way, that I was very willing to accept.

Just as Alex's lemonade stand and Anne-Marie's blog post led to possibilities they never imagined, Katharina's first Circle led to new ways that she and the growing WOL movement could make a difference. The new sponsors and partners made it possible to scale the movement much more quickly. She began organizing large annual conferences ("WOLCONS") to connect the community and inspire new people to join, and looked for ways to integrate WOL into existing programs. One was a culture change program for a Bosch division that allowed her to reach over four hundred employees in twenty-eight locations, and form over eighty new Circles.

Over time, Katharina became more confident and began making her work visible outside of the company too. She published posts on LinkedIn and delivered presentations at conferences,[3] and she started encouraging other companies to build their own WOL movements. Katharina joined a Circle with people from four other German companies (including Sabine from chapter 1, who was still in HR at Siemens at the time), and organized those companies and a few others into a WOL Community of Practice. They began to share their learning and host public WOL Conferences for practitioners in Germany and beyond, and their work together was featured on podcasts and in articles. They even won an HR Excellence Award for Employee Engagement and Collaboration, the first time it was ever awarded to a group.[4]

Another member of that cross-company Circle, Lukas Fütterer from Daimler, took advantage of the learning from Bosch and quickly grew Daimler's own movement. WOL was integrated into its global culture change program, which spread Circles farther in Europe, the Americas, and Asia. Daimler teamed up with Bosch to train an internal network of mentors who could help support and spread Circles globally, and the two companies worked together to organize a WOLCON for four hundred of their employees. On stage, wearing Working Out Loud hoodies, were board members from each company. Afterward, Daimler issued a press release with a quote from the head of their union, the Works Council.[5]

"Working Out Loud proves that the digital transformation does not need to instill fear and worry. It comes down to how it is designed. If you make your work visible, you also learn what it is worth. And if you network, you find additional possibilities of belonging and recognition," says Michael Brecht, Chairman of the General Works Council of Daimler AG. *"If 100 percent of all users of a new method have more fun doing their job, the method is right and makes work more humane. And as the works council, we can only support this."*

As I write this, the movement Katharina Krentz started at Bosch continues to expand. She recently traveled to Japan to train WOL mentors and spread Circles there. She spoke to reporters about Bosch's WOL movement at the company's annual meeting, right before the CEO's presentation. There are even WOL experiments in a Bosch factory, and a WOL program for HR managers around the world.

None of this has been part of a grand plan created by Katharina or the team. Rather, opportunities emerge with each step, and Katharina and her team make the most of them. Through a combination of passion, creativity, and persistence, the WOL Team at Bosch is now leading a rapidly growing movement of more than five thousand employees across fifty countries, and has inspired dozens of other companies to do something similar.

Q: I don't think a "movement" can change a company's culture. Change has to be driven from the top. You need to change the structures and systems, and only real leaders (i.e., top management) can do that.

Structures and systems absolutely matter, and executives do indeed have an outsized influence and authority over them. Yet, there are good arguments for why Katharina's movement can lead to a significant difference in the company's culture.

First, notice how Katharina's efforts, initially rejected, were ultimately embraced by the most senior managers in the company. Helping five thousand employees develop new skills and behaviors—and making those results visible—makes it more likely for executives to implement changes consistent with that movement. Remember the quote from Chip and Dan Heath in the epigraph for this chapter: "You've got to influence not only their environment but their hearts and minds." A change program will only make the difference you need it to make when you and your colleagues can *feel it*, when it's more than a set of posters on the wall or exhortations from an executive. When enough people experience that feeling, it becomes easier for management and structures and systems to change too.

A second argument is that even if structures and systems don't change right away, a critical mass of people exhibiting new behaviors can influence the remaining majority, and make the new behaviors the new normal. Researchers investigated this idea and published their findings as "Experimental Evidence for Tipping Points in Social Convention" in the journal *Science*:[6]

When the size of the committed minority reached ~25% of the population, a tipping point was triggered, and the minority group succeeded in changing the established social convention.

Finally, let's say you could not measure the effect of Katharina's movement on the company's culture. She still helped five thousand people develop new skills and relationships, and helped them fulfill their innate need for control, competence, and connection in the workplace. Even if you can't measure it, these changes will ripple out and affect the teams and projects throughout the company.

Q: I couldn't do this in our company.
We're too conservative.

When you're first starting out, think "lemonade stand" instead of "changing the culture of the company." For Katharina, thinking of changing four hundred thousand people at Bosch would rightly seem impossible. But finding four people for a Circle? That she could do.

Just as it happened at the music festival in the previous chapter, change happens when people feel something and want to share that feeling with others. You don't have to change everyone. You have to help a few and then make it possible for those few to help others. The movement almost always begins with a single person saying, "I want to try something different this time." Someone must take that initial step.

The first dancers

In my experience, what holds most people back from leading (and what held me back for most of my career), is not ability or opportunity or a boss. It's a voice in your head, a feeling that you need permission before acting, and a doubt that you are entitled to lead. *What if I get in trouble? Who am I to do this?*

Dealing with the first question is easier if you make your initial step small. No one gets into much trouble for setting up a lemonade stand. Dealing with self-doubt is trickier, and Kevin Kruse's assertions about leadership are good reminders.[7]

Leadership has nothing to do with seniority or one's position in the hierarchy of a company.
Leadership has nothing to do with titles.

Leadership has nothing to do with personal attributes. Leadership isn't management.

When you view leadership as a contribution, as doing something you feel is genuinely helpful for others, then of course you have the right to lead, and feeling that way makes it easier to take some kind of first step.

Vanessa North was the lone dancer in the Tax Office in Adelaide, Australia. (A tax office!) She had participated in a WOL Circle and liked it so much she scheduled an informal information session for her colleagues. She wrote me afterward to tell me how it went.

Forty-six people came, a few people couldn't come but still wanted to sign up, and a few heard about it afterwards. So ... Wait for it ... Out of 46 people who turned up I have 55 people signed up! So ... Drumroll please ... I calculate that as a 120% sign up rate. :-)

Larry Glickman in Buffalo Grove, Illinois, was the catalyst at the Union for Reform Judaism, which supports almost nine hundred congregations and has a million affiliates. After his experience in a Circle, he started to use an online community to spread the word. One Circle became two, then four, then fifteen, and they continued to spread. Congregations from different parts of the country began to ask about it. These early successes gave Larry the confidence to start writing publicly and give presentations about what he was doing. His most recent talk was to over two thousand people. "Working Out Loud became a term we used. Information was being shared in ways that really welcomed the input and engagement of others. Our organization had begun to work in a new way," he said.[8]

In Shanghai, Connie Wu said Working Out Loud helped her be more confident, and she started taking advantages of opportunities to make her work visible. After her Circle ended, she formed another one with people from a few different companies who had a presence in China. Less than a year later, Connie organized a team of volunteers to translate the guides into Mandarin, and partnered with a business school in Shanghai, her alma mater, to create an event "to help spread Working Out Loud in China." Why would she do this? Why would anyone follow her?[9]

People are Working Out Loud not just because we're fans of the method, but because we're hungry for a taste of what work could be like.

What are you hungry for?

I was visiting Niagara Falls with my family on a summer day, and to escape the heat we stepped inside to watch a short movie called *The World Changed Here*. It was only about six minutes long, but the title and the story of transformation reminded me of people in this book who are trying to make a difference.

In the mid-1800s, the land surrounding the falls was privately owned, mostly by companies using the fast-flowing water to power their mills. Public access was limited, and it looked some dystopian industrial wasteland. Landscape architect Frederick Law Olmsted (best known for designing Central Park in New York City) began to advocate for the preservation of the falls in the 1860s. Others joined him, and in time there were publicity campaigns using the social media of the time: newspapers and parades. Word spread, and a movement formed that gained the attention of the government. In 1885, Niagara Falls State Park became the first state park in the US.

Today, the falls are breathtakingly beautiful. The park is home to three hundred species of birds, and more thirty million people connect with nature there each year. There's still commerce, but it's in concert with the natural beauty and wonder of the falls, and there are now more than ten thousand state parks in the US, all made possible by a few people who cared, inspired others, and banded together to make a difference.

Some of the people in this section on leading have been inspired by big issues the world is facing. Others are hoping to improve the culture of their company, "hungry for a taste of what work could be like." All of them tapped into the intrinsic motivators described in chapter 2:

Control: I can take some action to change things. I am not powerless.

Competence: I am learning and improving, developing new skills.

Connection: There are others like me, and together we can make a difference.

What are you hungry for? Whether or not you lead a transformational change, there is beauty and power in the attempt, and I am inspired by those who have the courage to act. It is because of people like them we can say, "The world changed here."

All it takes is one person to start a movement. That person could be you.

KEY IDEAS IN THIS CHAPTER

- Leading a WOL movement inside your company is one way to experience what you and your network can accomplish together.

- The spread of WOL in an organization usually begins as a grassroots movement without budget or permission. A few early Circles help to test the idea.

- WOL can be the missing piece of most organizational change programs, helping employees to experience a better way of working and *feel* how it benefits them and the company.

- Anyone can start such a movement. Why not you?

EXERCISES

Something you can do in less than a minute

Do you believe that anyone can lead a movement that can inspire meaningful change? Or can change only come "from the top"?

Whichever you choose, how does your answer make you feel?

Something you can do in less than 5 minutes

Create a WOL group on your intranet. This is the place where you can link to the Circle Guides, or articles and videos about WOL, and share experiences from people inside and outside the organization. If a group already exists, use your five minutes to post something about your own WOL experience. It could be your thoughts about this book, or about your interest in starting a Circle, or asking if others might be interested in the topic.

If you don't work for an organization with an intranet, join the WOL groups on Facebook and LinkedIn, and post something there.

See if you get any responses, or find any second dancers for your movement.

22

Finding Your Ikigai

*In the culture of Okinawa, ikigai is
thought of as "a reason to get up in the morning."*

WIKIPEDIA

I FIRST HEARD the word *"ikigai"* in a talk about the secrets of living a longer, healthier life.[1] A team of researchers investigated communities around the world that had high concentrations of people one hundred years old or older. The talk was about nine factors that contributed to such longevity, including what people ate, how they exercised, and how they maintained their social connections. One of the locations was Okinawa, a string of islands at the southern tip of Japan, and one of the factors was a sense of purpose the Okinawans call their ikigai.

When I visited Okinawa, I could tell that life is more in balance there than in New York City, where I live, or even in Tokyo, where I've traveled often. There is less hurrying. The jobs may not pay as much as they do in the cities, but the people take pride in doing them well. They tend to eat local food that is in season, and families seem more connected to each other.

When the National Institute on Aging surveyed hundred-year-old Okinawans as part of the research, one of the questions was "What is your ikigai?" The longevity research showed that in one part of the main island there are five times as many centenarians as in the US, and people live about seven years longer than the average American. They're healthier too, experiencing only a fifth the rate of colon cancer and breast cancer as Americans, and less than a sixth the rate of cardiovascular disease.

Listening to the talk made me wonder, *What's my ikigai?* I had no answer to that question. I just had a nagging sense that there should be more to work and life. But more what? Money? Achievement?

"You are perfect just the way you are. And..."

I grew up believing that being content with the way things are is a sign of laziness. You should always be improving, focusing on the thing to be fixed or made better. So, I assumed that my purpose or happiness would be a destination of a kind, perhaps a particular job or lifestyle that would complete the sentence, "I will be happy when..." As I grew older, however, I began to see that this approach only leads to a life of never-good-enough, causing you to race toward a finish line that doesn't exist.

I came across a better philosophy in the work of Shunryu Suzuki, best known for founding an early and influential Zen organization in the US. In the late 1960s he lectured on "non-gaining mind," emphasizing practice for its own sake as opposed to some benefit in the future. He said the striving and clinging to expectations not only distorted your practice, but could also leave you miserable.[2]

You become very idealistic with some notion or ideal set up by yourself and you strive for attaining or fulfilling that notion or goal. But as I always say this is very absurd because when you become idealistic in your practice you have gaining idea within yourself, so by the time you attain some stage your gaining idea will create another ideal . . . Because your attainment is always ahead of you, you are always sacrificing yourself for some ideal. So this is very absurd.

A student asked Suzuki to clarify what he meant, so he simplified it:

You are perfect just the way you are. And there's room for improvement!

He may have meant it as a joke, but it made me wonder if such a paradox might be possible. What if you could accept yourself exactly as you are—and others exactly as they are—and still remain open and curious about further development? What if you could tap into all the benefits of personal development and improvement without the stress and drama?

Working Out Loud helped me find my ikigai, though it isn't what I might have imagined. My ikigai turns out to be less about changes to my life than changes to my approach to life. Over years of putting the five elements of WOL into practice, I am learning to contribute more and expect less, to offer more kindness and empathy instead of judgment, to be more purposeful and yet still curious. Most importantly, I am developing relationships that are daily sources of fulfillment, improvement, and opportunity. The WOL mindset allows me to have bigger ambitions while feeling more peaceful about trying to fulfill them. It makes for a more interesting life.

A month after being laid off, I set up my own company and called it Ikigai, LLC.

Finding your ikigai

No matter how old you are, the best years of your life can be in front of you, including possibilities you've never imagined. Your ikigai needn't be related to some far-off goal in the future, but how you approach every day. It can be the practice, not the result.

This idea was made clear to me in, of all places, a yoga class for newbies. The teacher, seeing the group striving and struggling to achieve a particular pose, encouraged us to focus on the practice, to pay attention to the doing without worrying about the outcome. She gave us advice that made me think about WOL:[3]

The practice is making the connections. That's it. Making connections that are meaningful and appropriate for you. When you do that, that's when you grow, when you reach places that are more significant for you.

My sincere hope is that the end of this book is a kind of beginning for you, and that as you practice Working Out Loud you'll find your own ikigai. Perhaps you'll craft your current job so it's more rewarding. Perhaps you'll write a new chapter in your life, or lead others to make a difference in your company or in the world. Perhaps you'll simply enjoy every day a bit more. "Whatever is meaningful and appropriate for you."

I wish you well.

Acknowledgments

HOW DO YOU acknowledge and thank thousands of people?

I need to begin with the hundreds who shaped this book and provided support and inspiration. The first person to see any part of it was Moyra Mackie, and she was so supportive that she inspired me to keep going. Eve Eaton suffered through many dry drafts and gently encouraged me to create something more personal. Eve's insights and friendship were a tremendous help throughout the years writing the book, and I continue to treasure them. Richard Martin, whom I had only spoken to once via Skype, generously offered hundreds of detailed comments and made me a better writer in the process. When he said, "This book will help a lot of people," I was inspired to work even harder.

Many people went to the trouble of providing written feedback on my unfinished, unpolished work. That's an extraordinarily generous thing to do. Thank you,

Kavi Arasu, Cornelia Bencheton, Helen Blunden, Jonathan Brown, Brigit Calame, Jacqui Chan, Bonnie Cheuk, Marie-Louise Collard, Dany Degrave, Cecil Dijoux, Brandon Ellis, Kathryn Everest, Mark Gadsby, Ravi Ganesh, Maddie Grant, Jessica Hale, John Harwell, Clay Hebert, Ken Hittel, Abigail Hunt, Christopher Isak, Harold Jarche, Irene Johansen, Lois Kelly, Guy Lipman, Anna-Clare Lukoma, Jackie Lynton, Victor Mahler, Jane McConnell, Stuart McIntyre, Ben McMann, Soon Min, Yavor Nikolov, Virpi Oinonen, Thomas Olsen, Vera Olsen, Martin Prusinowski, Päivi Räty, Carol Read, Greg Reilly, Perry Riggs, Kasper Risbjerg, David Robertson, John Rusnak, Samantha Scobie, Susan Scrupski, Ana Silva, Xavier Singy, Suellen Steward, Joachim Stroh, Lisette Sutherland, Kevin Sweeney, David Thompson, and Andrej Vogler. I owe a special debt to Eric Best, a former journalist and author of *Into My Father's Wake*, whose encouragement and editing of my early blog posts inspired me to become a better writer. There are many more people who contributed ideas, feedback, and support, and who read, share, and comment on my weekly posts. I extend my heartfelt thanks to all of them.

I owe a debt to all the people who worked with me on the individual coaching program and the first version of the Working Out Loud Circles. Patrick Arnold and Barbara Schmidt were the first people I coached, and I'll always remember their patience and encouragement. Mara Tolja formed the first London Circle with Anita Sekaran, David Griffin, and Anne-Marie Imafidon, and they shaped the very idea of what a Circle could be. My Barcelona Circle of Luciano Scorza, Carles Rodrigues, and Meritxell Martinez graciously helped me understand what worked and didn't work. My first Circle in New York City—Sharon Jurkovich, Nicola Harrison, and Melody Browne—helped me practice what I was preaching and turn it into a habit.

Then there are all the people I mention in the book who have inspired me with their stories. I'm honored to have learned firsthand from Sabine Kluge, Anja Rubik, Joyce Sullivan, Nikolay Savvinov, Paul Hewitt, Hayley Webb, Daniella Cunha Teichert, Mari Kotskyy, Bernadette Schreyer, and Vincent Kosiba. I learned too from those who served as more public examples, including Fred Wilson, Brandon Stanton, Jordi Muñoz, Bryce Williams, Jane Bozarth, Amanda Palmer, Austin Kleon, Alex Scott, Scott Berkun, Salman Khan, Tim Grahl, and Alycia Zimmerman.

There's a much longer list of people who spread WOL in different ways, and I appreciate all of them. Many tell a friend or share their experience on social media. Some have gone so far as to lead volunteer teams to translate the Circle Guides, like Tiago Caldas (Portuguese), Fiona Michaux (French), Connie Wu (Mandarin), Sebnem Maier (Turkish), Barbara Wietasch (Spanish), Marc Van De Velde and Annemie Martens (Dutch), and Teresa Arneri and Maria Chiara Guardo (Italian). Ragnar Heil and Jochen Adler played a key role in jump-starting the WOL movement in Germany, and now there are dozens of people organizing local WOL events in cities from Auckland to Vienna. In chapter 21, I mention the work of Katharina Krentz and Lukas Fütterer. I will forever be grateful to them and to the WOL Teams at Bosch and Daimler. Their impact on Working Out Loud cannot be overstated, and I am thankful for—and inspired by—all the WOL Teams that continue to build on what they began, and to the hundreds of people launching grassroots WOL movements in their organizations.

In the notes, I cited a number of researchers and authors who shaped my thinking. Two in particular changed my life: Keith Ferrazzi and Seth Godin. Keith's course came at a crucial time in my life and helped me see there was a better way to build relationships and discover opportunities. Seth's blog provides me with daily encouragement, so much so that I went up to him after one of his talks to thank him in person and ask for his autograph on a Seth Godin action figure. Embarrassing, but true. He signed it "Go make a ruckus."

I want to thank the team at Page Two Books, who brought this book to life and made it much better than anything I could have done on my own. Trena White, Gabi Narsted, Peter Cocking, Paul Taunton, Melissa Edwards, and Annemarie Tempelman-Kluit did a fantastic job of improving my writing, producing a beautiful book, and getting it into the hands of a global audience.

Finally, while most authors acknowledge their family's patience and support, my family has played a particularly important role. My children, Emily, Adrian, Olivia,

Hanako, and Hudson, all provide me with sparks of joy every day, and the youngest have literally grown up hearing about Working Out Loud. My wife Saori has endured all of my doubts, missteps, and emotional ups and downs. Her support, wisdom, and love have made it possible for me to do and be more than I ever thought possible.

Notes

Preface

1   The story of the five monkeys is thought to be inspired by a paper published in 1966, "Cultural Acquisition of a Specific Learned Response Among Rhesus Monkeys," by Gordon R. Stephenson et al. It's now passed on more as a business parable than as scientific fact. Just as we teach our kids about the Five Little Monkeys Jumping on the Bed so they won't hurt themselves, the story of the monkeys' learned helplessness is a cautionary tale meant to encourage people to be more mindful of what they're doing and why.

2   Connie Wu, "WOL Week—My Experience," LinkedIn post, November 16, 2017, https://www.linkedin.com/pulse/wol-week-my-experience-connie-wu.

Introduction

1   The video is just over nine minutes, and you can watch it on You-Tube: https://www.youtube.com/watch?v=XpjNl3Z10uc. Here's my own review of how it went: http://workingoutloud.com/blog//how-did-the-tedx-talk-go.

Chapter 1: Four Stories

1   Haufe Online, "Ehrung der 40 führenden HR-Köpfe 2019," July 11, 2019, https://www.haufe.de/personal/personalszene/die-40-fueh renden-hr-koepfe_74_430632.html.

2   Albert Sabaté, "Jordi Muñoz Wants You to Have a Drone of Your Own," ABC News, February 1, 2013, http://abcnews.go.com/ABC_Univision/ News/jordi-muoz-drone/story?id=18332163.

3   Chris Anderson, *Makers: The New Industrial Revolution* (New York: Crown Business, 2012), 146.

Chapter 2: Improving Your Odds

1   Studs Terkel, *Working: People Talk About What They Do All Day and How They Feel About What They Do* (New York: The New Press, 1974).

2   Bob Chapman and Raj Sisodia, *Everybody Matters: The Extraordinary Power of Caring for Your People Like Family* (New York: Portfolio/Penguin, 2015).

3   Terkel, *Working*.

4   Tony Schwartz and Christine Porath, "Why You Hate Work," *New York Times*, May 30, 2014, http://www.nytimes.com/2014/06/01/ opinion/sunday/why-you-hate-work.html.

5   Aaron Dignan, *Brave New Work: Are You Ready to Reinvent Your Organization?* (New York: Portfolio/Penguin, 2019), 8.

6   Maddie Grant and Jamie Notter, *Humanize* (Indianapolis: Que Publishing, 2011), 58.

7   Susan Sorenson, "How Employee Engagement Drives Growth," *Gallup Business Journal*, June 20, 2013, http://www.gallup.com/ businessjournal/163130/employee-engagement-drives-growth.aspx.

8   Amy Wrzesniewski, Clark McCauley, Paul Rozin, and Barry Schwartz, "Jobs, Careers, and Callings: People's Relations to Their Work," *Journal of Research in Personality* 31 (1997): 21–33.

9   Daniel H. Pink, *Drive: The Surprising Truth About What Motivates Us* (New York: Riverhead Books, 2011), 76.

10 Amy Wrzesniewski and Jane E. Dutton, "Crafting a Job: Revisioning Employees as Active Crafters of Their Work," *Academy of Management Review* 26, no. 2 (2001): 179–201.

11 Mark Granovetter, "The Strength of Weak Ties," *American Journal of Sociology* 78, no. 6 (May 1973): 1360–1380.

Chapter 3: The Evolution of "Working Out Loud"

1   Glyn Moody, "Thinking and Working Out Loud," *Open* . . ., September 20, 2006, http://opendotdotdot.blogspot.com/2006/09/thinking-and-working-out-loud.html.

2   Bryce Williams, "When Will We Work Out Loud? Soon!" TheBryces Write.com, November 29, 2010, https://thebryceswrite.com/2010/11/29/when-will-we-work-out-loud-soon.

3   "Social tools" include public social media platforms like Twitter and LinkedIn as well as enterprise social networks, such as Jive and Yammer, that are used internally for collaboration amongst employees.

4   You can see my video "What Is Working Out Loud?" on YouTube at https://www.youtube.com/watch?v=yOpgtC1JEzY.

Chapter 4: Purposeful Discovery

1   Alain de Botton, *The Pleasures and Sorrows of Work* (New York: Vintage, 2010), 113.

2   Bill Burnett and Dave Evans, *Designing Your Life: How to Build a Well-Lived, Joyful Life* (New York: Alfred A. Knopf, 2016), 114.

3   Brandon Stanton, "Humans of New York: Behind the Lens," *Huffington Post*, May 3, 2013, http://www.huffingtonpost.com/brandon-stanton/humans-of-new-york-behind_b_3210673.html.

4   Sarah Goodyear, "A 'Photographic Census' Captures New York's Characters," *The Atlantic Citylab*, April 20, 2012, http://www .citylab.com/design/2012/04/photographic-census-captures-new -yorks-characters/1816.

5   Stanton, "Humans."

6   Brandon Stanton, "I Am Brandon Stanton, Creator of the Humans of New York Blog," Reddit, May 20, 2013, http://www.reddit.com/r/ IAmA/comments/1eq6cm/i_am_brandon_stanton_creator_of_the_ humans_of_new.

7   Humans of New York, "We told her to sit with us so we could share her sadness," Facebook, August 8, 2014, https://www.facebook.com/ humansofnewyork/photos/a.102107073196735.4429.10209991 6530784/739242252816544.

8   Reid Hoffman and Ben Casnocha, *The Start-up of You: Adapt to the Future, Invest in Yourself, and Transform Your Career* (New York: Crown Business, 2012), 8.

9   Eric Ries, *The Lean Startup: How Today's Entrepreneurs Use Continuous Innovation to Create Radically Successful Businesses* (New York: Crown Business, 2011).

Chapter 5: Relationships

1   Nicholas A. Christakis and James H. Fowler, *Connected: The Surprising Power of Our Social Networks and How They Shape Our Lives—How Your Friends' Friends' Friends Affect Everything You Feel, Think, and Do* (New York: Back Bay Books, 2009), 31.

2   Dale Carnegie, *How to Win Friends and Influence People* (New York: Pocket Books, 1936), xix.

3   R.A. Hill and R.I.M. Dunbar, "Social Network Size in Humans," *Human Nature* 14, no. 1 (2003): 53–72.

4   Robin Dunbar, *Grooming, Gossip and the Evolution of Language* (Cambridge: Harvard University Press, 1996), 77.

5   This and the following quote are from Robert M. Sapolsky, *Behave: The Biology of Humans at Our Best and Worst* (New York: Penguin Press, 2017), 371.

6   Joseph Grenny, Kerry Patterson, David Maxfield, Ron McMillan, and Al Switzler, *Influencer: The New Science of Leading Change*, 2nd ed. (New York: McGraw-Hill, 2013), 271.

7   R.E. Kraut, S.R. Fussell, S.E. Brennan, and J. Siegel, "Understanding Effects of Proximity on Collaboration: Implications for Technologies to Support Remote Collaborative Work," in Pamela J. Hinds and Sara Kiesler (eds.), *Distributed Work* (Cambridge: MIT Press), 137–162.

8   Keith Ferrazzi, *Who's Got Your Back: The Breakthrough Program to Build Deep, Trusting Relationships That Create Success—And Won't Let You Fail* (New York: Crown Business, 2009), 41.

9   Clive Thompson, "Brave New World of Digital Intimacy," *New York Times Magazine*, September 5, 2008, https://www.nytimes.com/2008/09/07/magazine/07awareness-t.html.

10 Duncan J. Watts and Steven H. Strogatz, "Collective Dynamics of 'Small-World' Networks," *Nature* 393, no. 4 (June 1998): 440–442.

11 Brian Uzzi and Shannon Dunlap, "How to Build Your Network," *Harvard Business Review*, December 2005, http://hbr.org/2005/12/how-to-build-your-network/ar/1.

Chapter 6: Generosity

1   Meredith P. Crawford, "The Cooperative Solving of Problems by Young Chimpanzees," *Comparative Psychology Monographs* 14 (1937): 1–88.

2   Robert L. Trivers, "The Evolution of Reciprocal Altruism," *The Quarterly Review of Biology* 46, no. 1 (March 1971): 35–57.

3   Frans B.M. de Waal, Kristin Leimgruber, and Amanda R. Greenberg, "Giving Is Self-Rewarding for Monkeys," *Proceedings of the National Academy of Sciences* 105, no. 36 (September 2008): 13685–13689.

4   Adam Grant, *Give and Take: A Revolutionary Approach to Success* (New York: Penguin Books, 2014), 157.

5   Dale Carnegie, *How to Win Friends.*

6   Fred Wilson, "Writing It Down," AVC, September 19, 2013, https://avc.com/2013/09/writing-it-down.

7   Fred Wilson, "The Academy for Software Engineering," AVC, January 13, 2012, http://avc.com/2012/01/the-academy-for-software-engineering.

8   Reid Hoffman, "Connections with Integrity," *Strategy+Business* 67 (May 29, 2012), http://www.strategy-business.com/article/00104.

9   Keith Ferrazzi with Tahl Raz, *Never Eat Alone: And Other Secrets to Success, One Relationship at a Time* (New York: Crown Business, 2005), 21.

Chapter 7: Visible Work

1   Susan Cain, "The Power of Introverts," TED talk, February 2012, https://www.ted.com/talks/susan_cain_the_power_of_introverts.

2   Taken from the Penguin Random House reader's guide for *Quiet* by Susan Cain, which can be found at https://www.penguinrandomhouse.com/books/22821/quiet-by-susan-cain/9780307452207/readers-guide.

3   Andrew McAfee, "Do's and Don'ts for Your Work's Social Platforms," *Harvard Business Review*, September 28, 2010, https://hbr.org/2010/09/dos-and-donts-for-your-works-s.

4   Dave Winer, "Narrate Your Work," Scripting.com, August 9, 2009, http://scripting.com/stories/2009/08/09/narrateYourWork.html.

5   Brian Tullis, "Observable Work: The Taming of the Flow," June 25, 2010, Nextthingsnext.com, http://nextthingsnext.blogspot.com/2010/06/observable-work-taming-of-flow.html.

6   Bryce Williams, "When Will We Work Out Loud?"

7   The first and second stats are from James Manyika, Michael Chui, and Hugo Sarrazin, "Social Media's Productivity Payoff," McKinsey Global Institute, August 21, 2012, https://www.mckinsey.com/mgi/overview/in-the-news/social-media-productivity-payoff. The third is from Karen Renaud, Judith Ramsay, and Mario Hair, "'You've Got E-Mail!'... Shall I Deal with It Now? Electronic Mail from the Recipient's Perspective," *International Journal of Human-Computer Interaction* 21, no. 3 (2006): 313–332.

8   Bill French, "Email Is Where Knowledge Goes to Die," February 28, 2011, iPadCTO.com, http://ipadcto.com/2011/02/28/email-is-where-knowledge-goes-to-die.

9   Buurtzorg, "The Buurtzorg Model," https://www.buurtzorg.com/about-us/buurtzorgmodel.

10 Buurtzorg, "About Us," https://www.buurtzorg.com/about-us.

11 KPMG, "Value Walks: Successful Habits for Improving Workforce Motivation and Productivity in Healthcare," May 2016, https://assets.kpmg/content/dam/kpmg/pdf/2016/05/value-walks.pdf.

12 Frederic Laloux, *Reinventing Organizations: A Guide to Creating Organizations Inspired by the Next Stage of Human Consciousness* (Brussels: Nelson Parker, 2014), 80.

13 The collaboration platform is based on Jive software. You can learn more about it at https://www.jivesoftware.com.

14 You can read more about Mari at https://marikotskyy.com. You can find her album on iTunes at https://music.apple.com/us/album/rest/1389130759, and the RMN Classical compilation can be found at https://rmnmusic.com/call-for-piano-works-2019.

Chapter 8: A Growth Mindset

1   Claudia M. Mueller and Carol S. Dweck, "Praise for Intelligence Can Undermine Children's Motivation and Performance," *Journal of Personality and Social Psychology* 75, no. 1 (1998): 33–52.

2   Albert Bandura, Edward B. Blanchard, and Brunhilde Ritter, "Relative Efficacy of Desensitization and Modeling Approaches for Inducing Behavioral, Affective, and Attitudinal Changes," *Journal of Personality and Social Psychology* 13, no. 3 (1969): 173–199.

3   Albert Bandura, "Self-Efficacy," in V.S. Ramachandran (ed.), *Encyclopedia of Human Behavior 4* (New York: Academic Press, 1994), 71–81.

4   The Khan Academy mission can be found at https://www.khan academy.org/about.

5   Salman Khan, "Let's Use Video to Reinvent Education," TED talk, March 2011, http://www.ted.com/talks/salman_khan_let_s_use_video_ to_reinvent_education.

6   Jocelyn K. Glei, ed., *Maximize Your Potential: Grow Your Expertise, Take Bold Risks & Build an Incredible Career* (Las Vegas: Amazon Publishing, 2013), 79.

7   Ibid., 81.

8   Albert Bandura, "Cultivate Self-Efficacy for Personal and Organizational Effectiveness," in Edwin A. Locke (ed.), *Handbook of Principles of Organization Behavior* (Oxford: Blackwell, 2000), 120–136.

9   Seth Godin, "The Tragedy of Small Expectations," Seth's Blog, June 24, 2015, https://seths.blog/2015/06/the-tragedy-of-small -expectations.

Chapter 9: New Skills, Habits, and Mindset in 12 Weeks

1   Once you've finished this book, consider joining a WOL Circle. The structure, shared accountability, and peer support you'll experience in a Circle will make it much easier to practice. You can find more information at https://workingoutloud.com.

Chapter 10: A Practical Goal & Your First Relationship List

1   I wrote about an extreme example of this recognition phenomenon that I experienced. You can find it at https://workingoutloud.com/blog/why-is-italo-calvino-stalking-me.

Chapter 11: Your First Contributions

1   Scott Berkun, "#49–How to Make a Difference," ScottBerkun.com, October 2008, http://scottberkun.com/essays/49-how-to-make-a-difference.

2   Guy Kawasaki, *Enchantment: The Art of Changing Hearts, Minds, and Actions* (New York: Penguin/Portfolio, 2011), 102.

3   Reid Hoffman, "Connections."

Chapter 12: Take Three Small Steps

1   George S. Clason, *The Richest Man in Babylon* (New York: Signet 2002), 3.

2   Daniel Coyle, *The Culture Code: The Secrets of Highly Successful Groups* (New York: Bantam, 2018), 10.

3   Julia Rozovsky, "The Five Keys to a Successful Google Team," Re:Work, November 17, 2015, https://rework.withgoogle.com/blog/five-keys-to-a-successful-google-team.

4   Professional Learning Board, "What Is the SLANT Strategy and How Does It Improve Student Achievement?", https://k12teacherstaffdevelopment.com/tlb/what-is-the-slant-strategy-and-how-does-it-improve-student-achievement.

5   Sally Andrews, David A. Ellis, Heather Shaw, Lukasz Piwek, "Beyond Self-Report: Tools to Compare Estimated and Real-World Smartphone Use," *PLOS One*, October 28, 2015, https://journals.plos.org/plosone/article?id=10.1371/journal.pone.0139004.

Chapter 13: How to Approach People

1   Seth Godin, "The Sound of Confidence," Seth's Blog, November 23, 2013, https://seths.blog/2013/11/the-sound-of-confidence.

2   Dale Carnegie, *How to Win Friends.*

Chapter 14: Deepening Relationships Through Contribution

1   Barbara Schmidt, "A Whole New World," blog post, February 8, 2014, http://schmidtbarbara.wordpress.com/2014/02/08/a-whole-new-world.

2   Barbara Schmidt, "My Work Out Loud (WOL) Journey," blog post, July 7, 2014, http://schmidtbarbara.wordpress.com/2014/07/07/my-work-out-loud-wol-journey.

Chapter 15: Your Greater Purpose

1   Tony Grant and Jane Greene, *Coach Yourself: Make Real Change in Your Life* (New York: Basic Books, 2003), 17.

2   You can read more about Bernadette's journey at https://bernifox.com.

Chapter 16: The Start of Something Big and Wonderful

1   Leo Buscaglia, *Papa, My Father: A Celebration of Dads* (New York: Slack, 1989), 42.

2   Gregory Heyworth, "How I'm Discovering the Secrets of Ancient Texts," TED talk, October 2015, http://www.ted.com/talks/gregory_hey worth_how_i_m_discovering_the_secrets_of_ancient_texts/transcript.

3   This and the following quote are taken from David Griffin's blog post "Once Upon a Time," January 30, 2013, http://tellinstoriesblog.word press.com/2013/01/30/once-upon-a-time.

Chapter 17: Experimenting & Improving

1   Douglas Quenqua, "Blogs Falling in an Empty Forest," *New York Times*, June 5, 2009, http://www.nytimes.com/2009/06/07/fash ion/07blogs.html.

2   Jane Bozarth, *Show Your Work: The Payoffs and How-To's of Working Out Loud* (San Francisco: Wiley, 2014), 62.

3   You can find Nicola's style consulting business at http://www.harri son-style.com.

4   You can find Alycia Zimmerman's teaching site at http://www.alycia zimmerman.com.

5   Zimmerman's Scholastic articles and resources are available at https://www.scholastic.com/teachers/contributors/bloggers/alycia -zimmerman.

6   Peter Drucker, "How to Be an Employee," *Fortune*, May 1952.

7   You can watch this January 21, 2010, interview with Tom Peters, called "Brand You Thoughts from Tom Peters: Work on Your Writing," on YouTube video at https://www.youtube.com/watch? v=EEHLHd0PfWA.

8   Fred Wilson, "Writing," AVC, November 22, 2011, http://www.avc .com/a_vc/2011/11/writing.html.

9   Nicola Harrison, *Montauk: A Novel* (New York: St. Martin's Press, 2019), back cover copy.

Chapter 18: When It Doesn't Work Out the Way You Hoped

1   Tim Grahl, *Your First 1000 Copies: The Step-by-Step Guide to Marketing Your Book* (Lynchburg: Out:think Group, 2013), 84.

2   Amanda Palmer, *The Art of Asking: How I Learned to Stop Worrying and Let People Help* (New York: Hachette Book Group, 2014), 48.

3   Grahl, *Your First 1000 Copies.*

4   Seth Godin, "The Humility of the Artist," Seth's Blog, January 19, 2014, https://seths.blog/2014/01/the-humility-of-the-artist.

5   Seth Godin, "I Don't Like Your Work," Seth's Blog, March 2, 2019, https://seths.blog/2019/03/i-dont-like-your-work.

6   Dita Von Teese tweets under the handle @ditavonteese; you can find this post from September 6, 2010, at https://twitter.com/dita vonteese/status/23210190813.

7   PRI Public Radio International, "Ira Glass on Storytelling 3," You-Tube video, July 11, 2009, https://www.youtube.com/watch?v=X2 wLPOizeJE.

Chapter 19: Making It a Habit

1   Daniel Kahneman, *Thinking, Fast and Slow* (New York: Farrar, Straus and Giroux, 2013), 35.

2   You can read more about my habits experiments at https://working outloud.com/resources-for-week-8-make-it-a-habit.

3   Charles Duhigg, *The Power of Habit: Why We Do What We Do in Life and Business* (New York: Random House, 2012), 76.

4   Karen Pryor, *Don't Shoot the Dog: The New Art of Teaching and Training* (New York: Bantam, 1999), xii.

Chapter 20: Imagine the Possibilities

1   Kevin Kruse, "What Is Leadership?" *Forbes*, April 9, 2013, https://www.forbes.com/sites/kevinkruse/2013/04/09/what-is-leadership.

2   The original video, posted by Dkellerm on May 26, 2009, can be found at https://www.youtube.com/watch?v=GA8z7f7a2Pk. Derek Sivers popularized the video in his February 2010 TED talk "How to Start a Movement," which can be seen at http://www.ted.com/talks/derek _sivers_how_to_start_a_movement.

3   You can see a video of Alex and her family's June 2004 appearance on the *Today Show* at http://www.today.com/video/today/5136668#5136668.

4   Alex's Lemonade Stand Foundation, "Why We're Different," https://www.alexslemonade.org/about/different.

5   Brooke Lefferts, "How One Girl's Lemonade Stand Has Raised $80 Million and Changed Lives," *Today*, June 6, 2014, https://www.today.com/health/how-one-girls-lemonade-stand-has-raised-80-million-changed-2D79767939.

6   Alex's Lemonade Stand Foundation, "Where the Money Goes," https://www.alexslemonade.org/where-money-goes.

7   You can find KEA, which has a mission of "Kiwis Helping Kiwis," at https://www.keanewzealand.com.

8   Daniella Cunha Teichert, "My Personal WOL Moment: Getting Interest of Primary School Children in STEM-Related Subjects," LinkedIn post, October 8, 2017, https://www.linkedin.com/pulse/my-personal-wol-moment-getting-interest-primary-cunha-teichert.

9   Seth Godin, "The Tribes We Lead," TED talk, February 2009, ted.com/talks/seth_godin_on_the_tribes_we_lead.html.

10 Anne-Marie Imafidon, "The Case for Women Leadership in Technology and Beyond—My Month on the East Coast," blog post, October 31, 2012, http://aimafidon.com/2012/10/31/the-case-for-women-leadership-in-technology-and-beyond-my-month-on-the-east-coast.

11 This and the following two quotes from Anne-Marie Imafidon are from "For 2013: 3 New Year's Resolutions I Won't Have and 1 New Year's Objective I Do Have," blog post, December 31, 2012, https://aimafidon.com/for-2013-3-new-years-resolutions-i-wont-have-and-1-new-years-objective-i-do-have.

Chapter 21: Changing the Culture of Your Company

1   You can find out more about Bosch winning the XING New Work Award at https://newworkaward.xing.com/nominee/wol-co-creation-team-bosch.

2   Bosch, "Working Out Loud at Bosch," press release, February 1, 2018, https://www.bosch-presse.de/pressportal/de/en/working-out-loud-at-bosch-137280.html.

3   For example, in "How We Organize Working Out Loud at Bosch," Katharina describes her approach to spreading WOL, including a number of useful practices and survey results. You can find this June 15, 2015, post on LinkedIn at https://www.linkedin.com/pulse/working-out-loud-bosch-katharina-krentz.

4   Their entry for the HR Excellence Award was titled: "Working Out Loud: Self-Organized, Cross-Company 'Working Out Loud' Community of Practice." There were eight companies in the community at the time: Audi, BMW, Bosch, Continental, Daimler, Deutsche Bank, Telekom, and Siemens. It has since grown to include ZF and DHL. You can find information on their winning 2017 submission at https://www.hr-excellence-awards.de/gewinner-2017, and you can find photos of the winners on Twitter at https://twitter.com/i/moments/935249514142863361 and on LinkedIn at https://www.linkedin.com/feed/update/urn:li:activity:6340092528523563008.

5   Daimler, "DigitalLife@Daimler:Transformation of the Working World: Daimler and Bosch Hold the First Inter-Company 'Working Out Loud' Conference," press release, October 31, 2018, https://media.daimler.com/marsMediaSite/en/instance/ko/Digital LifeaDaimler-transformation-of-the-working-world-Daimler-and-Bosch-hold-the-first-inter-company-Working-Out-Loud-conference .xhtml?oid=41686666.

6   Damon Centola, Joshua Becker, Devon Brackbill, and Andrea Baronchelli, "Experimental Evidence for Tipping Points in Social Convention," *Science* 360, no. 6393 (June 8, 2018): 1116–1119, https://science.sciencemag.org/content/360/6393/1116.

7 Kevin Kruse, "What Is Leadership?"

8 You can watch Larry's talk on Vimeo at https://vimeo.com/267489708 and he wrote about it at https://glickmanonline.com/2018/05/25/ignite-out-loud.

9 Connie Wu, "WOL Week."

Chapter 22: Finding Your Ikigai

1 Dan Buettner, "How to Live to Be 100+," TEDx talk, September 2009, http://www.ted.com/talks/dan_buettner_how_to_live_to_be_100.

2 There is a translated transcript of Shunryu Suzuki's talk from April 13, 1967, at http://suzukiroshi.sfzc.org/dharma-talks/april-13th-1967.

3 You can find more wisdom from my yoga teacher, Mindy Bacharach, on her website: http://mindybacharach.com.

Additional Reading

I LOVE BOOKS. That feeling of anticipation you get when you open the cover and turn to the first page. How you can get immersed in a new world of ideas and insights. A good book changes you for the better.

Here are books I recommend that are related in some way to Working Out Loud. For a complete list of the books I read, search for my name at goodreads.com and add me as a friend.

A worldview

If you pick only two books from this list, pick these two. While I've always thought of myself as a positive person, these books freed me to be more joyful, and more open to the wonders in other people.

The Art of Possibility: Transforming Professional and Personal Life, by Rosamund Stone Zander and Benjamin Zander

Are You Ready to Succeed? Unconventional Strategies to Achieving Personal Mastery in Business and Life, by Srikumar Rao

New approaches to basic skills

With the help of these three books and a lot of practice, I've become better at the fundamental skills of writing and presenting. And I'm convinced anyone can do the same.

On Writing Well: The Classic Guide to Writing Nonfiction, by William Zinsser

Presentation Zen: Simple Ideas on Presentation Design and Delivery, by Garr Reynolds

Resonate: Present Visual Stories That Transform Audiences, by Nancy Duarte

Developing relationships

These books made me think more deeply about what people need and want in relationships, and how we can improve our everyday communications with others.

How to Win Friends and Influence People, by Dale Carnegie

Never Eat Alone: And Other Secrets to Success, One Relationship at a Time, by Keith Ferrazzi, with Tahl Raz

Who's Got Your Back: The Breakthrough Program to Build Deep, Trusting Relationships That Create Success—And Won't Let You Fail, by Keith Ferrazzi

Nonviolent Communication: A Language of Life, by Marshall B. Rosenberg

Personal productivity and creativity

These are shorter and easier to read than most of the other books, and gave me a new perspective on how people create great work and also make it visible.

Manage Your Day-to-Day: Build Your Routine, Find Your Focus, and Sharpen Your Creative Mind, edited by Jocelyn K. Glei

Maximize Your Potential: Grow Your Expertise, Take Bold Risks & Build an Incredible Career, edited by Jocelyn K. Glei

Steal Like an Artist: 10 Things Nobody Told You About Being Creative, by Austin Kleon

Show Your Work! 10 Ways to Share Your Creativity and Get Discovered, by Austin Kleon

Show Your Work: The Payoffs and How-To's of Working Out Loud, by Jane Bozarth

Why we do what we do—and how to change it

A better understanding of how our mind works is perhaps the most empowering knowledge you can have. These books helped me understand what generally motivates people and how to change our habits. They also empowered me to actively shape my future, instead of just watching it unfold.

Thinking, Fast and Slow, by Daniel Kahneman

Your Brain at Work: Strategies for Overcoming Distraction, Regaining Focus, and Working Smarter All Day Long, by David Rock

Self-Esteem: A Proven Program of Cognitive Techniques for Assessing, Improving and Maintaining Your Self-Esteem, by Matthew McKay and Patrick Fanning

Mindsight: The New Science of Personal Transformation, by Daniel J. Siegel

Flow: The Psychology of Optimal Experience, by Mihaly Csikszentmihalyi

Drive: The Surprising Truth About What Motivates Us, by Daniel H. Pink

The Willpower Instinct: How Self-Control Works, Why It Matters, and What You Can Do to Get More of It, by Kelly McGonigal

Behave: The Biology of Humans at Our Best and Worst, by Robert M. Sapolsky

Work and management

These books about work and the workplace gave me hope that we can make work better for everyone. Each offers very human ways we can realize more of our individual and collective potential.

Everybody Matters: The Extraordinary Power of Caring for Your People Like Family, by Bob Chapman and Raj Sisodia

The Culture Code: The Secrets of Highly Successful Groups, by Daniel Coyle

Working: People Talk About What They Do All Day and How They Feel About What They Do, by Studs Terkel

Work Rules! Insights from Inside Google That Will Transform How You Live and Lead, by Laszlo Bock

Creativity, Inc.: Overcoming the Unseen Forces That Stand in the Way of True Inspiration, by Ed Catmull and Amy Wallace

Reinventing Organizations: A Guide to Creating Organizations Inspired by the Next Stage of Human Consciousness, by Frederic Laloux

Driving larger-scale changes

Whether you're trying to change your company, change your local community, or change the world, these books offer approaches, frameworks, and heroic examples that will inspire you and make you more effective.

The Lean Startup: How Today's Entrepreneurs Use Continuous Innovation to Create Radically Successful Businesses, by Eric Ries

Influencer: The Power to Change Anything, by Kerry Patterson, Joseph Grenny, David Maxfield, Ron McMillan, and Al Switzler

The Dragonfly Effect: Quick, Effective, and Powerful Ways to Use Social Media to Drive Social Change, by Jennifer Aaker and Andy Smith, with Carlye Adler

Switch: How to Change Things When Change Is Hard, by Chip Heath and Dan Heath

Linchpin: Are You Indispensable?, by Seth Godin

Mountains Beyond Mountains: The Quest of Dr. Paul Farmer, a Man Who Would Cure the World, by Tracy Kidder

The Blue Sweater: Bridging the Gap Between Rich and Poor in an Interconnected World, by Jacqueline Novogratz

Whatever It Takes: Geoffrey Canada's Quest to Change Harlem and America, by Paul Tough

Finding happiness

The insights found in this eclectic mix of books allowed me to see the limitations I had placed on myself. They showed me the different ways I was actively making myself unhappy, and how I could change them.

Designing Your Life: How to Build a Well-Lived, Joyful Life, by Bill Burnett and Dave Evans

Steering by Starlight: The Science and Magic of Finding Your Destiny, by Martha Beck

The Happiness Project: Or, Why I Spent a Year Trying to Sing in the Morning, Clean My Closets, Fight Right, Read Aristotle, and Generally Have More Fun, by Gretchen Rubin

Be Free Where You Are, by Thich Nhat Hanh

Peace Is Every Step: The Path of Mindfulness in Everyday Life, by Thich Nhat Hanh

Zen Mind, Beginner's Mind: Informal Talks on Zen Meditation and Practice, by Shunryu Suzuki

Taking the Leap: Freeing Ourselves from Old Habits and Fears, by Pema Chödrön

A New Earth: Awakening to Your Life's Purpose, by Eckhart Tolle

Into the Magic Shop: A Neurosurgeon's Quest to Discover the Mysteries of the Brain and the Secrets of the Heart, by James R. Doty

About the Author

JOHN STEPPER helps organizations create more open, collaborative cultures—and helps individuals access a better career and life—by spreading the practice of Working Out Loud, a peer support method that re-humanizes work. Individuals learn to build relationships that make them more effective and give them access to more possibilities. Companies get intrinsically motivated behavior change—new skills, habits, and mindset—at scale. The WOL movement has spread to over sixty countries and to a wide range of organizations. John has delivered a TEDx talk about the movement and writes about making work better at workingoutloud.com. He lives in New York City.